BOOK TWO

EMILIO

QUINN RYDER

SANTOYO BROTHERS TRILOGY

Copyright

This book is a work of fiction. Names, characters, places, and incidents are either products of the author's imagination or are used fictitiously. Any resemblance to actual persons, living or dead, business establishments, events, or locales is entirely coincidental. The author makes no claims to, but instead acknowledges the trademarked status and trademark owners of the following marks mentioned in this work of fiction.

Editor: Ryder Editing and Formatting

Proofreaders: Courtnay Gray

Cover Design: Sweet 15 Designs

Printed in the United States of America

First Edition: April 2021

Library of Congress Cataloging-In-Publication Data has been applied for

Ryder, Q

Emilio-The Santoyo Brothers Trilogy Book Two – 1st Edition

ISBN: 9798500524522

ASIN: B08RX9ZT66

Synopsis:

I've been in love with Esmeralda Barrio, since my father brought her home sixteen years ago, bruised, broken, and empty. For the last sixteen years I've watched her change from the beautiful girl I fell in love with, to the cold-hearted woman I no longer recognize. Living under my father's rule has hardened her, and now she's just as bad as he is, treating others with the cruelty that was once shown to her.

I never expected to be next in line to take over the familia, but now that my brother is on the lam and in bed with our enemy, I have no choice but to step into the role that was meant for him. That role came with a prize I never expected—Esmeralda. Now she's mine to own, something I had wished for since I was a young boy when I watched her love everyone in my family but me.

Falling in love with the woman covered in scars was incredibly easy for me, but getting her to love me back has proven to be the most difficult task I've ever had to face. Now that I know the truth behind our union, I'm determined to save her from herself before it's too late. She has something my father wants, and if I don't stop him, I might just lose her forever. I've always been the one to run away from danger, but now that I own Esmeralda's hand, I'll do anything to protect her, even if it means giving up my own life for hers.

Dedication

This book is dedicated to Michele...
She's the woman who saw Emilio's worth before he found it himself. I hope you are ready for the Latin lover that's ready to sweep you off your feet in the pages that follow.

Trigger Warning:

This book contains dark themes, violence, and situations that may be triggering for some readers. If there are certain triggers that may be hard for you to read, this book may not be your thing.

Prologue

The rain pelted heavily against the frosted glass of my bedroom window. I often found myself staring out into the darkness, especially when it rained. Rain was like the sky's filthy tears, leaking out its emotional baggage as it poured down from the heavens above, soaking its weak-minded subjects below.

It was raining the night he brought her home. I still remember that day very vividly. It was the first time I had ever seen someone covered head to toe in blood. Well, that I remember. I was there the night my mother died; I was told she was covered in blood too, but I don't remember anything about it except the toy truck I held in my hand. It was the only trinket that I had to link me to my mother, and since her death, she had been the only woman who ever mattered to me until Esmeralda was thrown into my life nine years ago.

Six Years Ago

There was a commotion in the living room. My father's men rushed through the doors, each of them looking pale and streaked in blood. The rain had washed most of it off their bodies, but remnants still lingered behind. It was obvious they got into some heavy shit.

Most people didn't pay attention to me. I was the brother that was the most overlooked, the one my father felt had no future in the Familia. I couldn't shoot like my older brother, Sergio, and I wasn't picked on and verbally abused like Mateo, my youngest brother.

Emilio

My father wasn't a warm, caring soul. He was meaner than a badger in heat and would put a bullet hole in your head if you dared to cross him. He was a vindictive bastard and always had something up his sleeve. You could barely call him a father with how horrible he was to his children. But even though I was the one he felt could never amount to anything, I still didn't get half the crap Mateo did. I'm pretty sure that kid has been broken down and beaten more times than I'd like to count. Nobody says shit about it, except for Sergio, he always steps in to protect Mateo and me from our Father's wrath. I don't know what it is about Mateo that makes my father hate him so much. Sure, his eyes are blue instead of brown and his hair is a lighter shade than ours, but that shouldn't be a reason for our father to mistreat Mateo so badly.

"Make way, Waif!" one of the men shouted at me, pushing me to the side with his big beefy hands. I didn't even know he saw me standing there until I was being thrown against the wall.

A few seconds later, my father comes rushing in, carrying a girl in his arms. She looked to be about my age and was covered in blood from head to toe.

"Capo, what do you want us to do with her?"

"We need to save her, Jorge. She's the key to everything. Find the doctor. Bring him here immediately."

Jorge nodded, quickly exiting the room in search of Juan, our resident doctor on call. I may have been young, but I wasn't stupid. I knew my father did bad things. He had a way of commanding a room and making them all cower in fear.

I crouched and hid under a table, watching the scene play out as my father's men stood around him, gawking. "Out, all of you!" he shouted.

The men cleared the room, leaving my father and the bloody girl alone. He didn't know I was watching, or what I heard that night. But I heard everything, every damn dirty word that left his sadistic lips. His hand cupped her cheek, thumbing the large gash that split her face from her ear to the corner of her lips. Then that thumb went lower, tracing down her neck, until his hand was almost covering her breasts.

"You are meant for my son, Esme. You will make him a fine wife someday, but your body is just too beautiful. That's why those men disfigured you the way they did. Your beauty was stolen away from you at too young of an age."

I didn't know what he meant; I couldn't see a thing from where I was hiding. The doctor entered the room, checking the lifeless girl that laid so helplessly in my father's lap.

"She not dead," the doctor said in broken English. "But she won't live if we don't fix her up or get her to the hospital."

"No hospitals. This needs to happen here," my father barked, snapping the doctor immediately into action.

The next hour was spent washing her body free of blood and cleaning her wounds. I watched it all from my hiding place, entranced by the girl my father had brought into our home in the middle of a rainstorm.

After they were done fixing her up. The doctor and my father left her on the couch to recover. She was now dressed in a single slip-on that covered her filleted skin.

I crawled across the ground until I was kneeling beside her. She hadn't opened her eyes at all during the cleanup, and if I didn't see the faint movement of her chest rising and falling with each strangled breath, I would have thought she was dead.

For some reason, I felt compelled to take her hand, staring at her bandaged face and wondering how anyone could damage something so beautiful. She would definitely have a scar, one that would make her look like a monster, but I saw past it all, I saw the beauty that lurked beneath her marred features. I'm quite certain that was the moment I truly fell in love with Esmeralda Barrio. I was drawn to her vulnerability and helplessness. An enormous need to protect her overwhelmed my tiny body. She was my age, but here she was, lying on the couch, cut up and butchered, instead of in a hospital where she belonged.

Maybe if I had paid more attention to that tiny little fact, what happened later on would've made more sense to me. Instead, I focused on my feelings, and squeezed her hand as I whispered, "I don't know if you can hear me, but I wanted to let you know that you're safe now. I'm here to protect you."

I barely felt her fingers as they twitched to life and gave my hand a limp squeeze.

Turning her head, she let out a giant gasp. Her eyes were ladened with tears, each one individually marked with fear and pain. She didn't need to speak to tell me that she was haunted. Her hollow gaze did all the talking for her. But when she finally realized that she was no longer in danger, her beautifully bruised and battered lips hissed out, "¿Se han ido las Monstruos?" **Are the monsters gone?**

<div align="center">~~~</div>

I often wonder if I could've done anything to change the way Esmeralda saw me. We grew up together, hanging out and playing like two friends who were always destined to be. As she got older, she became even more beautiful to me, but she wasn't mine to have… she was Sergio's. My father immediately betrothed them the second she started living with us, and it was like Esme robotically complied like a dutiful slave. Though she was never treated like one, I could see the restraints my father placed on her. She wasn't allowed out much, and if she was, it was only with him or Sergio. Pretty soon it became obvious that Esme was being hidden from prying eyes.

A part of me wanted to believe it was because of her scars, but something in the back of my mind told me that my father was hiding her for his own selfish reasons. It wasn't until later that I finally found out what the secret behind Esmeralda Barrio truly was. And when I did, it was the first time I had ever thirsted to spill someone else's blood… my father's.

Chapter One

Present Day

"He's gone." The words were both cruel and satisfying to say out loud. Watching my father's face drop into an angry scowl when he realized that his "favorite" son had yet again disappointed him, forced me to hide my smile.

Sergio was lucky my father didn't kill him when he found out he was sleeping with Catalina, but the old man was determined to marry off Esme to my brother and bring her into the family. His urgency was a little disturbing and had me wondering if the old man had a reason behind speeding up their nuptials?

"What do you mean he's gone?" My father's voice was so loud that it carried through the church, straight back to the room where Esme was preparing to get ready.

The doors swung open, and she emerged, stealing my breath the moment she walked out in that long, flowing white dress. Her scars were covered by a thin veil, and she stood at the end of the pews, staring at my father and me with confusion in her eyes.

"Where's Sergio?" she asked, looking around the church.

"He's gone," I repeated, knowing those satisfying words were now turning cruel. The last thing I'd ever want is Esme to be hurt, but I also couldn't lie to her. She meant way too much to me for that.

"This is ridiculous," she yelled, marching up the aisle without her song, or the flower girl placing a trail of petals before her. "First that asshole sleeps with another woman, then he runs off so he can stand me up at the altar?" Tears pooled in her fawn colored eyes, as emotion and betrayal hit her. "It's my face, isn't it? No man would ever want to be tied down to this ugly face."

My father tried to cover up the mild look of pain in his eyes. Only my brothers and I knew what they did behind closed doors, and I wasn't entirely certain that my father's feelings for her went beyond spreading her legs every other night.

"Why does this always happen to me?" Esme cried, dropping to her knees in a puddle of sorrow.

The priest joined us, whispering under his breath something to my father.

After a few moments, my father's back stiffened. A cold scowl crossed his face as he brought Esme up from the ground.

"Stop that," he ordered her. "You're getting married today. I paid for this damn wedding, and somebody is fucking going to say I do, or else I'm going to be taking the money I lost out in someone's blood."

Esme's smile brightened a little as she looked at my father with hopeful eyes. It made me sick to see her staring at him with a look of adoration he didn't deserve. The man was far from a saint, and he took advantage of her when she was at her weakest, promising her the world, when he only had plans to keep her shut in where no one could see her.

"Does that mean what I think it means, Julio?"

My father smirked, shifting his eyes to the priest that stood stoic beside him.

"Of course, it does…" his voice trailed off. "Emilio will make a perfect husband for you."

"What?" I questioned in shock, completely unprepared for his announcement.

"Yes, you're going to marry Esme instead. Problem solved."

"NO!" Esme wailed. "I can't, Julio. Why can't we just be together?" she begged, clutching his shirt for support.

He stepped away from her, looking around the empty room to make sure no one heard that but us.

"Shut up, Esme, and keep your tongue. The lies you tell are going to do more harm than good, so be a good girl and stand up there with your future husband. The priest has a ceremony to start."

"But, Padre…"

My father answered my words with a slap across the face. "Do this, Emilio. I've already had one son break my heart today, I don't need another. Family before blood. Remember?"

I rubbed at my cheek, knowing that I couldn't talk my father out of this, so as I stood there at the altar, watching the priest go through his repetitive tongue, I couldn't help but silently thank my estranged brother for giving me this opportunity.

Because of his love for Catalina, I'm able to marry the woman of my dreams. It would be a happy memory if it weren't for my wife weeping beside me like a leaking mannequin.

"I now pronounce you man and wife. You can kiss the bride?" the priest said with hesitation, knowing that Esme hadn't stopped crying since my father broke the news.

I turned to her, ready to kiss my beautiful bride and take that first step of being married to the woman I love, but she turned away, fleeing down the aisle away from me.

My father laughed, knowing damn well he still won this battle. "Looks like you got some work cut out for you, Mijo. Why don't you go deal with her? I need to phone an old friend and enlist his services."

"Who?"

"Let's just say that your brother isn't the only one famous for being a contract killer. El Planchazo is a fucking kitten compared to the monster that is Mr. X."

"Padre, no! He'll kill Sergio…"

My father sneered. His lip curling in amused disgust.

"So what? He made his choice. *Familia antes que sangre.* Family before blood. He betrayed the family and now he will pay in his blood."

Chapter Two

I found Esme out on the front steps weeping into her dress until black tears created streaks that soaked through the painfully white fabric. It was a color of purity—a color a woman like Esme should never wear.

Esme lost the purity in her soul long ago. I'm not exactly sure when she changed, she'd always been sweet to me, but then something inside her broke. That fragile shell I met when my father brought her home in the rain, was repaired with spikes and cold metal. She hardened, becoming as cruel as my father. She still treated me like we were best friends when no one was watching, but when she was around my brother or father, she treated me like they did, shitty.

"Hey…" my voice trailed off as I watched her crumble before me. "I didn't mean for this to happen, Esme."

"Fuck you," she hissed. "Don't stand there and act like you didn't want this, Emilio. You've always wanted me. I see the way you look at me. It fucking broke your heart that I never touched you like I touched them. Well, I hate to break it to you, but you still aren't touching me now." Her words were as sharp as daggers, and each one sliced through me, creating even more friction between us.

I didn't know how to calm her down or how to react. What I did know was that I needed to find a way to calm the devil living inside of her and bring back the angel I missed with every beat of my heart.

My mouth opened, ready to soften her sobbing when I felt him push past me.

"Get the fuck up!" he ordered. "You're making a scene."

Esme's head shot up, staring at my father with hurt in her eyes. "Why couldn't you just marry me?"

My father's mustache twitched, a clear sign he was hiding something. "Because I don't want another wife."

"Another?" I questioned, looking at him strangely.

"Yes, Mijo, another. I'm still married to your mother in my heart." My father threw out his wedding ring long ago. He didn't give two fucks about my mother. She was just another trophy for him to shine and polish to make himself look good.

Esme stood up, then immediately she began pummeling his chest with angry fists. "I fucking love you!" she screamed. "I fucking have done everything you ever asked of me. Why do you treat me like I'm trash that you can recycle and use over and over again?"

My father gripped her wrists forcefully, his narrowed eyes slicing through her, penetrating her with all the hostility brewing inside of him. "I could never love a monster like you, Esme. The only thing pretty about you is your pussy. Why do you think I always fuck you from behind? It's so I don't have to look at your hideous face. I can continue picturing I'm fucking a gorgeous woman that way."

She crumbled to the ground, defeated by my father's harsh and painful words. Somewhere deep down inside of her, she actually believed he loved her. But my father doesn't love... he takes and uses. Since the day I was fucking born, all I have ever seen him do is burn everything he touches to the ground. He was one of the most feared men in Mexico City, and people cowered and bowed at his feet like the serfs he made them out to be. You weren't anything to my father unless you proved your worth. That's why Sergio leaving hit him so hard. My brother had perfect aim. He was the hitman most men dreamed of hiring. Then he went and fell in love with the enemy, leaving my father and the kingdom he was going to pass down to Sergio behind.

You don't cross Julio Santoyo, but that's exactly what Sergio did. Now my father wanted his head on a spike—his own flesh and blood.

"Pick up your filthy wife and take her on your honeymoon. When you get back, we have business to discuss." My father thrusts plane tickets in my hands, and sneers. "When she gets back, she'll be in my bed again. But you can have your fun with my dog for a week, she is your wife after all."

Every cell in my body was ready to lash out. If I was a stronger man, I could've reached out and grabbed his throat, squeezing the life out of his cold dead eyes. But I'm not a strong man... I'm Emilio, the one that doesn't matter—the weak one. And like the dutiful son I am, I bow my head in surrender and say, "Yes, Padre."

Chapter Three

The plane's tires hit the landing strip of the small airport deep in the heart of the Bahamas. It was a beautiful place to celebrate my union to Esmeralda, but she hadn't said a single word to me since my father left her on the steps of the chapel. It was almost as if she was a walking corpse, zombified to the bone from all the pain and suffering my father had caused her. I hated seeing her this way, but she wouldn't let me in. Hell, she wouldn't let me take her bags or help her off the plane.

"I can do it myself," she snapped, swatting my hand away.

I watched in amusement as she struggled to carry her luggage, barely able to put it in the awaiting taxi. The taxi driver attempted to smile at us, but I could see his confusion. We were far from a happily married couple. The only thing we were, was married. Happiness seemed like a wish that would never be granted to either of us.

I spouted off the address for the little house my father rented for us for the week and settled into my seat. Esmeralda sat as far away from me as she could, staring out the window as silent tears streaked down her pitiful face. There was no masking her misery. She didn't paint on a happy face for others to see. Her emotions were raw and broken, just like her.

"So, what brings you to the Bahamas?" the driver asked from the front seat.

"We got married yesterday," I answered, stealing a glance at my miserable bride.

I could see him eyeing us through the rearview mirror. Questioning if I held her at gunpoint to marry me. Maybe I did, even if I wasn't the one holding it to her head. I was the catalyst that started everything. I couldn't watch my brother suffer the way he did. That's why I unlocked the door to his room, left the car running in front of the chapel, and aided him in his escape. He didn't love Esme, and the last thing I wanted was for him to be forced to marry someone he didn't love—someone I loved with every beat of my heart.

I knew what I did was dangerous, but I had to. It was the only way he could be with Catalina. Besides, I couldn't watch him marry Esme, it would've broken me. If my father ever found out that I betrayed him, I'd be dead—my father wouldn't hesitate to pull the trigger.

"Does she know?" the driver questioned, pulling me out of my wayward thoughts.

For the first time since marrying me, Esme smiled, and then an amused snicker bubbled out of her chest. "Unfortunately," she grumbled.

"Arranged marriage?" the man asked.

"You could say that," I answered him, wondering why marrying me was the end of the world to her. If she only knew how deep my love for her ran, how good she would have it if she just let me love her like I want to.

Our driver goes into some big detailed story about how his older brother had been in an arranged marriage. I pretty much let him drone on as I tuned him out, thinking about how I could change Esme's perspective of me. But I had nothing.

"… and then she killed him."

My eyes popped open the second the driver's words left his lips.

"Wait, the girl your brother married killed him?" I asked, my head shooting up to look at him.

"Yup, stabbed him in the chest nine times. One time for each girl he stuck his dick in. The bitch was ruthless. She took her life after it happened, slicing her own wrists, and bled out next to his body. Nobody found them for nine days. Kind of ironic… they got married on the ninth of September, in the year 1999. Even more ironic is the fact that they said I do around nine in the morning. I don't think I've hated a number more than the number nine. It's the number that ultimately did my brother in."

A number. How could a number be someone's demise? It was ridiculous when you thought about it, but I guess anything can have an impact on someone's life—even a number.

"Serves him right," Esmeralda said, speaking softly beside me. "Men are evil bastards that don't know what they have sitting right in front of them. The world would be better off without any men in it."

My eyes carefully migrated to where she sat. She was still looking out the window, staring at the scenery as it whipped past the car.

She was so goddamn beautiful. She was mine, but she wasn't, and I vowed in that moment to show her just what I saw in front of me… a woman who was broken and needed to be pieced back together. She was a complex puzzle that this puzzle master was ready to take apart and configure. Even if some of the pieces were broken or missing, I was determined to show Esme just how much she meant to me. I'd put her back together or die trying.

Chapter Four

The bungalow my father rented was gorgeous. It was a small one-bedroom home with a vast state-of-the-art kitchen, a huge bathroom with a jacuzzi tub, and a balcony that overlooked the ocean. We even had our own private beach. It was the perfect place to escape life and have a romantic week away with the woman you love. Only my woman refused to look at me. She didn't want me touching her or even thinking about her. It was almost as if she was repulsed by the thought of me touching her.

I didn't think I was that bad of a guy, but Esme acted like I was a venomous snake ready to bite her or a pesky spider she wanted to squash.

"This is beautiful," I remarked, setting our bags in the bedroom. I stared at the four-post king-sized bed adorned with a gold and red duvet, imagining our first night together. Would she fall asleep curled up in my arms? Would she let me make love to her as the sun set until it rose the next morning?

"You can sleep on the floor or the couch," she ordered before walking into the bathroom and shutting the door.

I wouldn't see her again until dinner time.

When she found me later, I was sitting out on the balcony, watching the ocean waves as they crashed and overlapped each other. I was lost deep in thought, wondering how I ended up married to someone who would never love me back.

"I'm hungry," she said, breaking me free of my wayward thoughts.

"Okay. What would you like to eat?"

"I don't know. Anything at this point."

I stood up, staring into her amber eyes, getting lost in the lingering tears that still shined faintly in them.

Did she cry the whole time she was in the bathroom?

She hid behind her hair, allowing her long black tresses to cover the scar on her face. She was always hiding behind a shield of hair—afraid to have others look at her only physical flaw. It was atrocious. Who ever gave it to her did it so no one would ever think she was beautiful again. They carved out the side of her face, creating a gash three inches wide that had been sewn back together haphazardly. It was raised and pulled at her full, tender lips, creating a permanent sneer she'd always have.

"Stop looking at me like that," she demanded.

"Like what?"

"Like you think I'm beautiful."

"But you are…"

Her hand flew up, slapping me viciously across the face. "You're as bad as your father and brother. It's like the Santoyo men were born liars. Don't fucking pity me with your false compliments, Emilio. I'm just a dog, remember? WOOF, WOOF!" she screamed at me before turning away.

I wasn't sure what to say, so I just stayed silent, wondering if there was anything I could do to change her mind, but the hatred in her eyes told me she wasn't ready to listen to my truths—she could only believe the lies that festered in her head.

"Come on," I told her, pulling on her arm gently to follow me.

"Where are we going?"

"We're going to take a walk and find something to eat."

I didn't stop to see if she was following me, I knew she was. The entire time we walked in silence, strolling down the beautiful street toward the small epicenter of the city.

We came to a stop in front of a store that sold books, and she looked up at it with longing eyes.

"Do you want to go in there first?"

"They look closed."

The sign on the door said open even though the lighting inside was dim. I walked up to the door and pushed it open, showing her inside the store.

"Welcome," the shopkeeper said from behind the counter. "I'm closing in about five minutes, so make it quick."

Esme strolled around the bookstore, running her fingers across the leather binding of each book. She stopped in front of the romance section, grabbing a few reads from off the shelf, then kept walking until she got to the journals.

"I've always wanted to keep a diary," she stated mindlessly. She wasn't exactly talking to me, but she was at the same time. I noticed that was kind of normal for her. To talk to herself while talking to others around her.

There was a certain journal she stared at with longing. It was a leather-bound journal with a gold lock and a single key. She picked it up, turned it over, and grimaced when she saw the price. Reluctantly, she placed it back down before she stopped to pay for her books at the counter, and quickly left me and the shopkeeper inside.

"She seems sad," the older woman stated.

"She is."

"Why?"

"Because she was forced to marry me, and she didn't want to."

The woman nodded and got up, walking over to where the journal was that Esme was looking at.

"You give this to her. Someone that sad needs an outlet to get out their pain. My husband makes these, that's why they are so expensive. He binds them himself. It's a painstaking process. But love is put into each and every journal he makes. She looks like she needs all the love she can get." The woman hands me the journal and a pen with a fluffy ball at the top, before she smiles.

"Love her even when she won't let you. That's the secret to a successful marriage."

"Thank you," I replied, taking the book from her. "And I will… always have."

She patted my hand one last time, before following me to the door and locking it behind me.

Esme was standing in the middle of the sidewalk, staring at nothing but everything all at once.

"Here, the shopkeeper wanted you to have these."

Esme looked up, staring at the journal and pen in my hand.

"Why?"

"She said you looked sad and someone that sad needed an outlet to get out their pain. So, she handed me the journal and pen. Her husband makes the journals. She said he puts love into each and every one he makes."

Esme takes the journal and pen away from me, her face expressionless. "I doubt I'll even use it."

I nodded. "And that's okay. It's here if you want it, though."

She didn't say a word after that. Instead, she led me down the street, stopping at a small bar near the docks.

"I want to get drunk."

"Okay," I replied, following her into the bar.

For the next three hours, I watched in silence as Esmeralda drank everything she could get her hands on. She fed herself in between drinks to keep from vomiting, but it was almost like she wanted to get alcohol poisoning. By her tenth drink, I paid the tab and practically carried her from the bar. There was no way she'd make it back home walking. She could barely keep upright. So, I flagged down a cab driver and by the time we made it home she was asleep.

Carefully, I pulled her out of the cab, paid the driver, and carried her back into our bungalow. She moaned softly in my arms, her hands gripping my shoulders tightly as she nestled against my chest. For the first time since we said I do, she was actually letting me hold her. Sure, she was drunk as all hell, and had no idea I was touching her, but at least I got to hold her on our wedding night, even if it was for only a few minutes.

I laid her gently on the bed, covering her with blankets, then quietly crept towards the door. I was only a few steps away when I heard her stir behind me.

"Get it over with," she grumbled.

I stopped, turning around slowly. She was still laying on the bed, but she had removed all her clothing, legs spread open as she stared at me blankly.

"Esme, what are you doing?"

"One of the stipulations of us being married is that we have to consummate our union. Fucking you has to happen in order for our marriage to be official. I know that much about marriages." She opened her legs. "So, go ahead. Fuck me, Emilio. Get it over with so I never have to fuck you again."

Anger boiled inside of me like searing liquid. In a furious rage, I stomped across the room until I was on the bed, crawling across her naked body and staring directly into her cold, uncaring eyes.

She gasped at my forcefulness, not expecting me to stalk across the room and overpower her like I did. Grabbing both of her wrists, I pin them above her head. I could feel her breasts pressing against my chest, and the warmth of her pussy through my tented pants. Normally, it would've affected me, but right now I was fuming with pent up rage. Seeing her naked like this had always been one of my dreams, but she was fucking ruining it with her bitter and pissy attitude.

I dipped down so my breath whispered against the slope of her neck and she could feel the bulge in my pants rubbing against her needy core.

"Let's get one thing straight, Esmeralda. I may want you more than I have ever wanted any woman that I've had in my bed, and I may crave your body like I'm dying of thirst and starving for my last meal, but I won't, for one fucking second, take your beautiful body unless you're goddamn begging for it. I'm not here to appease some fucking piece of paper. When we consummate this union, it's going to be because you've fallen in love with me. I'm not the kind of man that fucks and forgets. I'm not my brother or my father. When I finally make love to you, every stroke, every thrust, every lingering kiss I place on your beautiful lips is going to be filled with passion and wanting need. The moans you scream and the shuddering breaths you take will all be mine. You're going to give yourself to me willingly. You won't treat our union as some throwaway fuck that you'll be done with ten minutes later. You'll obsess over it until you're on the verge of madness, Esmeralda. When I'm done making love to you, you'll never have to think of another man ever again because you'll be too busy moaning my goddamn name every agonizing second we're apart. I'm going to own you just like you've owned me since we were seventeen fucking years old."

Her eyes widened as her chest heaved wildly. I could see the desire burning in her eyes. A man had never spoken that way to her before. Inebriated or not, she could feel the fiery desire burning between us, and whether she liked it or not, I just lit the match that created an inferno of chaos that's blown up her tiny little world.

I didn't dip down and claim her lips like I wanted to, and my hands didn't run down her body and feel every inch of her skin that was kissed by erotic goosebumps. No. I did none of that. Instead, I pushed myself off of her, exiting the room before she had a chance to say another word, leaving her alone and naked on our wedding night like the cruel bitch deserved.

Chapter Five

I woke up to the smell of bacon and eggs cooking in the kitchen. The couch was lumpy and left a nagging crick in my neck. The dreams I had of Esmeralda last night also left me with a bad case of morning wood. At least in my fantasies she wanted me, but unfortunately, I was left to live in the cruel reality of being married to a frigid bitch that would rather fuck my father or brother than ever touch me.

"Buenos Días," her voice sang from the kitchen.

I briefly looked up and caught her watching me, her eyes perusing my naked torso, staring at the lack of definition while she wetted her lips. I wasn't built like my father or older brother. Sergio had muscles for days and my father was built like a goddamn tank. Mateo and I both were on the scrawnier side of the gene pool, but I was taller and lankier, and Mateo was scrawny and half my size.

If I was any other man, I would've asked her if she liked what she saw, but I was me, and the man I am is the kind that brushed off her blatant gawking and took a seat at the small dinette.

For a few minutes, I analyzed her movements in the kitchen, watching as she flitted from one side to the other, preparing our meal.

She loaded a plate with food and put it in front of me, then immediately dropped to her knees.

"What are you doing?"

"What I always do every morning." In one swift movement, her hand snaked up the leg of my shorts, gripping my still semi-hard cock.

I jumped, pushing away from the table. "Esme, what the fuck are you doing?"

She challenged me with a glare and the roll of her eyes. "I fucking told you, I'm doing what I always do every morning."

"And what exactly is that?"

"I prepare Julio or Sergio breakfast, depending on who I stayed with the night before, then suck his cock while he eats."

Bile rose in my stomach as I pictured her servicing my father and brother like a cheap whore or sexual slave.

"Get up!" I practically yelled.

"Why?"

"Because I'm not my father or brother. Get yourself a damn plate of food and sit across from me at the table. We're going to eat together."

She cautiously rose to her feet. "A real man would've taken the blow job. It was kind of like a gift for not taking advantage of me last night. I thought you were being a gentleman, but now I see that you're half the man your father and brother are." Her snide comment had my fists clenching by my side. I vowed that I would never hit a woman, but Esme's fucked up attitude had my palms itching to break that rule.

Anger seared my veins like hot venom. In two quick steps, I had closed the distance between us, invading the personal space she worked so hard at maintaining. When she wouldn't look at me, my hand shot out, fingers digging into the skin of her cheeks and squeezing as I jerked her head to look at me. I didn't hurt her, but I damn sure let her know I wasn't going to be walked all over either. Her doe colored eyes flashed with both regret and submission. And for a second, I kicked myself for making her feel weak. That second came and went when a cold sneer crossed her beautiful lips, and she smacked my hand away.

"Go ahead and hit me. I bet you slap like a fucking bitch."

"Let's get one thing straight, Esme. A real man would never hit a woman and treats her with fucking respect, not like some fucking dirty doormat he can wipe his feet on. You'll never be my subservient dog. You will always be my equal. As long as you treat me with respect, I'll do the same to you. But if you want to act like a raging bitch and try to provoke me, you're barking up the wrong tree. Don't expect me to be pissing rainbows and all smiles, but you can expect me to treat you like a human being. Now get your plate, sit your fucking ass down, and eat."

She opened her mouth wordlessly, then clamped it shut with pursed lips. She had nothing to say, but I was also out of words myself. I wasn't sure why she was so fucked up, but I was determined to chip through the frigid layers of bitch to find out.

After a few seconds of standing there just staring at me, she walked to the kitchen, grabbed a single piece of bacon and a small spoonful of eggs, and sat down.

"Is that all you're going to eat?"

She took a few cautious bites, then shrugged. "The only thing I have going for me is my figure. My face is hideous and all the beauty I used to have was sliced away by the bastards who did this to me. I only put in my body what will keep it slim."

It was the first time she had opened up to me. It might have only been a tiny sliver of her reality, but in this one breakfast I was learning more about her than I expected.

"What?" she asked, when she caught me staring at her.

I shook my head, shoveling a bite of food in my mouth. "It's nothing."

"No, what?"

I placed my fork on the plate and dotted the corners of my mouth with my napkin. I had already finished my food and was too distracted by her strange eating habits to ask for more. This way if she got hungry later, she'd have something to eat.

"Esme, I've always thought you were beautiful, even with your scar."

"Why?"

"Because your scar may have sliced into your flesh, but it didn't pierce your soul. To others, that scar is a flaw, but I see it for what it really is—your power. You went through a tremendous amount of hell that night, and you came out still breathing. That's some fucking powerful shit. Scars are badges of courage and the battle wounds of your soul. You fought a battle that day that you weren't ready or capable of fighting. Your scar is nothing more than a reminder of the strength and courage that kept you going that night. It may have created an imperfection on your beautiful face, but only people with lying eyes see your scar and nothing else. I see past it… I see everything you are and everything you can be. I just wish you could see yourself in the same light."

I suddenly lost my appetite. "I think I'm going to go take a shower. Maybe later we can go for a walk on the beach?"

She didn't answer me. She just sat there like a statue, pushing her eggs around with her fork mindlessly.

Without saying another word, I rose from the table, placing my dirty dish in the sink, then headed for the bathroom. When I turned around to ask if she brought a bathing suit, I saw her wiping away a few loose tears. Somehow, my words had broken through a thin layer of ice surrounding the wall she put up around herself. I knew it wouldn't be enough to pull her out of the world she'd become so accustomed to, but it was a start. Now I just needed to find a way to thaw the rest of her before it was too late, and she let her self-loathing consume her until she turned to dust.

Chapter Six

Dear Abuelita,

How's heaven? Did you welcome Madre, Padre, Pico, and Jose with open arms? Sometimes I wonder if I was meant to join you all in heaven. I find myself questioning why God spared me that night. Why he chose me to continue living in this cruel world, scarred by the demons who were out to destroy me.

I was left to live with the memory of watching my parents and brothers die and the residual fists I always feel beating on my body like unwanted ghosts. They cut away my beauty, stole my innocence, and fractured my soul all in one night. Was this God's plan? To watch one of his children's souls, get ripped from existence at the hands of selfish men? I vowed that night I would never let another man touch me, but I broke that vow. I let him into my bed... then I let his son in between my legs ... and now... now I'm nothing more than a shell inside myself, married to a man that's too good for me.

Julio broke me, Abuelita. I didn't think it was possible for a man to shatter emptiness... but he did. He forced me to marry his son, but still expects me to end up in his bed every night, even though he told me he only thinks of me as a dog he fucks.

I don't know why I find it easier to be fucked and used than worshipped and loved. I have too much hate and vengeance in my heart to sit by and allow someone in—especially a Santoyo man.

The only people I ever loved were taken away from me too early. The final squeeze of your hand as you took your last gasping breath is something I'll always remember, just like the sound of gunshots popping off as my family was executed right in front of my eyes. Those visions still hover around me, like the smell of your churros right after you coated them in sweet sugar and left them on the counter for me and my brothers to eat. The cinnamon wrapped into my nostrils and stayed there for weeks. Sometimes, I feel like it enters my senses like a whisper of a ghost. It's the same whisper I hear when I stand on the edge of the cliffs looking over the ocean, the one telling me not to jump. It's your voice isn't it, Abuelita? It's you who keeps me from ending this miserable life I've been forced to live.

The only reason I'm still here is because of you... because of them... because of all the Barrios family that died at the hands of an unknown enemy. I won't stop living until I find the men who took the lives of my family. Then, and only then, will I walk up to that cliff and throw myself into the ocean waves crashing below, joining you all in heaven once and for all.

Until then, I'll enjoy the memories I shared with you and hang on to the hint of cinnamon lingering in my mind. It's all I have left, Abuelita. Everything else inside of me is gone.

Siempre te amaré,

Esme

Chapter Seven

I never meant to read the journal. It just so happened that she left it out on the balcony, unlocked. I had only meant to open it to see if she actually used it, but when I saw the entry on the first page, I couldn't stop reading. Her words were vague, but it seemed like Esme felt she didn't deserve to be loved.

I wish I knew how to change her mind without incriminating myself, but there was no way to do that without letting her know I was invading her thoughts.

One thing I did pick up while reading was her love for churros. My own abuelita had passed down her recipe to me long ago. It was one of my specialties. Tonight, I'd make her a four-course meal with all the Mexican staples, just like my abuelita would do for us every Sunday. Then, after everything was done, I'd take her for a stroll out on the beach, underneath the stars and moonlight, and spend some quiet time with her.

We'd pretty much avoided each other all day. When I was inside, she was out on the balcony. When I went outside to look at the ocean, she took her leave and went in to shower. It was almost as if she was avoiding me and knowing her innermost thoughts told me why. She was pushing me away, and because I was a determined man, I wasn't about to let her.

A few hours later, she came padding into the kitchen wearing only a sheer white cover and a black bikini. The contours of her body had every bit of my attention. She had the perfect hour-glass figure, complete with voluptuous breasts, widened hips, and legs that my cock ached to be between.

If I could give Esme a glimpse at what being loved by me would entail, she'd never want to slide into my father's bed again. I was a master at love, even if I didn't look like it on the outside.

It wasn't known by many, but while my brother grew up learning how to perfect the art of shooting a gun, I was instructed on how to woo a woman in the bedroom. My father, being the fucked-up asshole he is, felt that each of his sons needed to know what it was like to be a man by sixteen. By the age of sixteen, I was nowhere near ready to have sex, but my father insisted on it and took me to Tijuana for the summer. He left me in a whore house with one of his side chicks by the name of Juliet. She was the madam of Las Chicas Bandidos, the best whorehouse in Mexico. At first, Juliet had me sweeping and running small maintenance on her property, but after a few weeks of living with her, Juliet had other plans for me that didn't involve brooms and hammers.

"Emilio, ¿alguna vez te lamiste un coño?" **Have you ever licked a pussy before?**

I stared at the older woman, wondering if I lost my mind. But I didn't.

"No," I told her, shaking my head.

"Have you ever touched one before?" she asked me in broken English.

"No."

"Louisa! Get in here now!"

A few seconds later, a young girl entered the room. She couldn't have been much older than me, maybe eighteen or nineteen. She was beautiful, with long black hair, eyes that looked like rich caramel chocolates, and a nice trim body that was free of any fat.

"Louisa is my youngest girl. She's also my least experienced. You will both learn together..."

"Learn what?" I asked her.

"How to make love," Juliet answered as if it was the easiest thing to comprehend. "Now, Louisa, remove your clothes."

Louisa bowed her head in shame, removing the thin dress that barely covered her skin. She was marred by the marks of other men. Bruising from sucked kisses ran up her neck, while the remnants of welts and fingerprints left a trail down her torso.

"I found Louisa on the streets, naked and abused by a group of men. I took her in like I would my own daughter, but every soul here has to pay their way. She knew that when she came here. Though, she's not worth a penny until she knows how to please a man. Don't worry, I've had her checked, she's clean. Judging by your innocent face, I don't have to worry about you giving her anything bad."

I stared at the woman, then my gaze dropped to the beautiful girl before me.

"Now, Emilio, the easiest way to please a woman, is to bring her to an orgasm with your tongue and fingers. Louisa, come lay on the bed."

Louisa crossed the room, sliding across the bed until her head was on the pillow next to Juliet. She didn't seem the least bit shy, even though the older woman was lying next to her half naked—tits hanging out of the top of her dress, as she played with the girl's hair.

"Emilio, come here."

I was afraid to move. It was like my feet were part of the floorboards and the only thing moving was my inexperienced cock that seemed to be twitching in my pants.

"NOW!" she barked, snapping my attention back to her.

I crossed the room, stopping at the foot of the bed. Juliet grabbed Louisa's left leg and pulled it, so she was exposed and her pretty pink pussy was on full display.

The bed was almost as big as the room. It could've easily fit five people on it, but in that moment, it felt like the smallest bed in the world as I climbed up on the satin sheets and crawled closer to the two women.

"We shall start with something easy. First, you must take off all your clothes."

The embarrassment I felt as I stripped in front of them was maddening. I wanted to run, but I was also very curious. When all my clothes were shed, both women had smiles that practically touched their ears.

"You're bigger than I imagined. You should see some of the cocks that come through here, they're Vienna sausages compared to the monster between your legs. Yes, you will definitely help Louisa learn how to properly service a man."

"What do you want me to do?" I practically stuttered.

"You're going to eat Louisa's pussy until she orgasms on your tongue."

My eyes practically flew out of my head.

"Don't worry, we'll work up to it. I want you to crawl over her and kiss her, Emilio."

I had never kissed anyone before, so as I crawled over Louisa, my flaccid cock brushing over her entrance, I could feel my nerves as they traveled through my body, creating shaky limbs and uncontrolled quivers that quaked through my core.

That first touch of our lips was like magic. Every cell in my body fired at once, and as she opened her mouth to invite me in, I could feel my cock roaring to life between us, rubbing against her center as it begged for a taste. I was so into that first kiss that I didn't even notice Juliet's hand traveling up and down my back, it was like I was numb to everything around me—everything but Louisa.

"Good, you kiss well, Emilio. I can see the passion burning in her eyes and the way her body melts into you, it won't take you long to bring her to the edge. You're going to trail those sweet kisses down her body, following her neck until you reach her chest. The chest is an important part of seduction. Nipples are sensitive little shits; they're easily pleased and aroused. You haven't even started yet and her breasts are swelling with need. Do it, kiss down her body."

I glanced up at Louisa, wondering if she wanted me to do this. She gave me an encouraging smile, her gaze penetrating me with a deep carnal desire. It was all I needed to keep going. My lips carried their way down her body, stopping at her swelled breasts just like Juliet told me. Once there, I didn't wait for commands, I took her nipple into my mouth and gently bit the tip as I swirled my tongue around her budded nip.

Louisa's fingers dug into the silk sheets, her moans going from quiet whimpers to screaming moans of ecstasy. I felt Juliet slide her hand in mine, then guide it down Louisa's body until my hand was touching the most intimate part of her. It was like I was born to make love, because my fingers were playing with Louisa's pussy like they already had the movements mesmerized. She bucked and arched her body beneath me, her gasping breaths becoming even more fervent as my lips worked their way down to her throbbing pussy.

"You want to take this slowly, Emilio. Most men think that aggression and speed will take a woman over the edge. Those men are wrong. It's the art of the tease that sends women spiraling. You go slow, make her body beg for that release, then when you can feel her writhing beneath you in complete submission, that's when you attack."

I acted out every damn action she asked of me, rolling my tongue against Louisa's clit, thrusting my fingers inside of her warm pussy slowly at first, then as I felt her squeezing me on the inside, and her moans erupted and morphed into erotic screams, I increased my pace, both with my tongue that licked and lapped at her center, and the fingers that drove everything inside her to that edge. Feeling her orgasm was invigorating but tasting her sweet cum was what blew my mind.

After that, Juliet paired me and Louisa every night, practicing any move she could teach us. Louisa and I became so in tune with each other's bodies, that we never realized that we had fallen in love. It came suddenly, as if one day I woke up realizing that I couldn't live without her. When the summer days ended, and it was time for me to return to Mexico City with my father, I was determined to bring Louisa back with me, Juliet and my father be damned. I had everything planned out. The entire conversation had already been written in my mind. I was going to tell my father that she was pregnant, which she wasn't, and that it was my child and responsibility. All that changed the second my father showed up on the brothel steps.

"Let's go, Emilio," he ordered, barely looking up from his phone.

My birthday had come and gone over the summer. I was now officially a man. Old enough to drive a car, man enough to make a woman weak in the knees, and finally brave enough to tell my father exactly what I wanted.

"Padre, I'd like you to meet mi corazón, Louisa. I'd like her to return home with us."

My father looked Louisa up and down, then scoffed in disappointment. "She's fucking fat and ugly; I have no room for more dogs in my house. Let's go Emilio."

Louisa already had tears in her eyes. She was far from fat or ugly, but my father took happiness as a sign of weakness, and the fact that I wanted to be with her made me weak in his cold, unforgiving eyes.

"Padre, you don't understand." I took a step forward, placing a loving hand on Louisa's stomach, smiling with all the love and adoration I had in the depths of my soul. "Louisa is carrying my child—your grandchild."

Whatever my father was looking at had his full attention. He didn't look up nor did he acknowledge what I had said.

"I said let's go, Emilio." The authority in his voice would crumble the strongest man. I could already feel the nerves in my body shaking my core. Louisa was even worse, she was sobbing against me, pleading in broken English for me to stay.

"Please don't go, Emilio. I love you."

"I love you too, Mi Corazón, I promise I'm not leaving you." I took a deep breath, ready to challenge my father's blatant brush-off of me and the woman who was my whole world. "JULIO!" I screamed, finally getting his damn attention. "Did you not fucking hear me? I said she's fucking pregnant with my damn child. I'm not leaving her. I don't care what you say. She's coming with us."

My father's eyes narrowed on me, finally settling on Louisa's stomach, disputing my lie with his judgmental eyes. I was expecting him to say something, I thought he'd at least give in to my demands and bring her along with us. But I should've known better. My father's vindictive nature was a hellacious beast hell bent on creating havoc wherever he went.

For a split second, his eyes softened. He opened his arms as if he was accepting her into the family. "Louisa, my darling girl, are you in fact carrying my son's child within your womb?"

She looked at me nervously, taking a deep breath as she took a few steps forward, as if she was walking straight into his embrace.

"Yes, I am."

My father's smile was full of false hope. To an outsider, he looked welcoming and happy. To those who knew him best, like me, we could see it for what it really was, fake, calculated, and downright unimpressed.

BAM!

Louisa's warm body hit the ground in a cold-heartless thud. My father's movements were so fast that I barely blinked before he had the gun out and was squeezing the trigger.

A single gunshot wound pierced her flesh, creating a perfect bullet hole right between the eyes. There was no surviving that shot. I knew that the second the pool of blood seeped from her lifeless body.

I dropped to my knees, ready to cradle her defiled beauty in grief, but before I had the chance, my father's massive hand had me by the shirt and was dragging me toward the car. He didn't look up from his phone as he walked past his men. There was zero emotion other than dominance as he bit out the words, "Clean that mess up and pay the fucking wench for her lost girl. Make sure my son doesn't try anything stupid."

My father entered the vehicle, and one of his men pushed me in behind him. Once the door was shut and locked from the outside, I was stuck in the back of the car with my father, the man who wouldn't even look up from his phone after killing the woman I loved in cold blood.

Emotion attacked me like a vicious leopard starved and ready to eat. Each tear was like a pint of acid that burned its way down my cheek and what was left of my fragile soul.

"Why?" I whispered, my voice hoarse and choked with emotion.

This time he looked up, as if taking Louisa's life wasn't already enough of a punch. "Because women make you weak, and no son of mine is going to be tied down to a no-good, fat, ugly whore. Besides, she wasn't even fucking pregnant. I've seen the sparkle in a woman's eyes when she's with child three times in my life. That bitch only saw dollar signs and freedom from that whore house she lived in. I did her a fucking favor by ending her miserable existence, Emilio. She wanted freedom, now she has it. The freedom to rid this planet of her putrid filthy stench. Wipe those disgusting tears from your eyes and man the fuck up. I fucking did you a favor, Mijo."

"How?"

"Because now you know what it's like to have loved and lost. It will strengthen you. It will strip you of all that pitiful weakness and put some fucking hairs on that puny chest. I'm making you a man, Emilio. You've learned how to seduce a woman, now you need to learn how worthless they really are."

My father's cruel words were always stuck in my head. Somewhere in his past, a woman had betrayed him to the point of having a blatant disregard for anyone with tits and a pussy. He didn't give a fuck about the women that frequented his bed. There wasn't a single ounce of remorse in his deranged and damned soul. He was a fucking monster, one that had ruined every woman that ever came into my life. Louisa was just the beginning of his tormented twisting of my love life. Now he had thrown Esme in my path, giving me exactly what I wanted, but dangling her like a carrot in front of my starving eyes. I was starved for her—starved for the affection she refused to give me.

So, as I prepared the epic meal that I had made with her in mind, I prayed to anyone up in the sky looking down on me for help. I needed it. Because even though this was just another one of my father's demented plans, I had plans of my own.

By the time we returned to Mexico, Esme would officially be mine. She would never return to my father's bed, and if he tried, I'd put a bullet between his eyes, and another in his heart. The first shot would be for Louisa, the second would be for any heart that he decimated over the years with his ruthless vindictive ways. Because if he was cold enough to break his own son's heart over and over again, then there had to be at least a million lost and broken souls wandering endlessly in the sea of his vicious wake.

Chapter Eight

"What are you doing?" Esme asked when she came into the kitchen and found me in the middle of making our meal.

"I like to cook when I have time. My abuelita taught me how to make a hearty Mexican meal before she died. Please sit. For our first course, I have made some pico de gallo, salsa, and guacamole to go with these homemade tortilla chips." I placed the basket of chips and homemade dips in front of her and walked back into the kitchen.

"Why do I smell cinnamon?"

"Oh! That's our dessert, I'm just finishing them up. I hope you like churros."

Her eyes lit up in a way I'd never seen them do before. "I adore them, but I haven't had them in years. I was too afraid they'd ruin my figure."

"Esme, you're my wife now. I don't care what kind of figure you have. Every pound on your body will be beautiful because you're beautiful. Fat, thin, short, tall, none of that matters to me, I'll always see you as what you are... a pure display of feminine perfection."

She blushed. "Sometimes it seems like you know exactly what to say and do to make me question my initial thoughts about you."

"And what thoughts were those?" I finished frying up the churros and placed them on a paper towel. Then I dipped and rolled them in the cinnamon sugar mixture and placed each churro on a plate, piling it high until they almost toppled over. One by one, I carried each dish to the table, until the entire thing was covered in delicious food. Not only did I make everything from scratch, but I was sure the enchiladas I made were going to win her over.

"That you were useless and worth nothing."

"You sound like my father."

A haunted look crossed her gaze as she carefully bit into a chip. "I do, don't I?" She sighed. "He's a very powerful man and that power can cross oceans it seems. I'm sorry."

I looked up from my plate of food mid bite. "For what?" I asked in a muffled response.

She giggled, ignoring my blatant display of shitty manners. It's hard to stay civilized when food this good is sitting in front of you.

"For what I've said the past few days. It's not so bad being married to you. You're nice… I guess I'm just not used to nice men."

I nodded, knowing her words went past my father and Sergio. They traveled back to that day in the rain, the day my father carried her in half-dead and bleeding.

"It's okay. I know I wasn't your first choice."

She shook her head. "I've never had a choice since the day I moved into your family's home. I wouldn't know what thinking for myself is if I tried."

Pondering her words, I smiled. "I have an idea. How about tomorrow we do anything you want; it doesn't matter what it is. You get to call all the shots tomorrow. Every decision and choice will be solely yours."

"Really?"

"Yes. I told you, Esme, I take this marriage as an equal partnership. Your thoughts are my thoughts. Your wants become my needs. I'm here for you through the good and the bad, and for better or worse. My vows were one hundred percent genuine, even if my father caught me off guard and forced us together. When I love a woman, I do it with every fiber of my soul. Those fibers are the woven immortal threads of the God's, you can't sever something that is built to live forever."

"You speak like a poet… like someone who has so much to give but has lost everything at the same time."

"I have lost a lot in my lifetime."

"Besides your mother, what have you lost?"

Taking her slender hand, I grasped it over the table, my dark gaze penetrating those warm pools of caramel that curl around her iris. "I have only been in love two times in my life. Once, when I was sixteen, and once when I was seventeen when a bloody and broken girl was carried into my home in the middle of a rainstorm. Her lifeless body was so helpless and lonely. She laid on my floor barely breathing, and she stole my heart the second I saw her shallow and shuddering breaths gasping erratically as she fought to hold onto what was left of her life. I could see the strength in her face, even with it being bruised and mangled by the war she had fought before arriving. I vowed that night that I would always protect her and take care of her, and I'm determined to keep that promise Until I'm the one no longer breathing."

Emotion leaked out of Esme as she weakly squeezed my hand. One tear fell down her cheek, tiptoeing around her scar as it found a path onto the tablecloth below. Another followed and another until her quiet sobs shook her entire body.

"I don't deserve someone as sweet as you, Emilio."

Moving out of my chair, I dropped to a knee, gently lifting her chin until she was looking me in the eye.

"Don't you get it, Esme? You deserve more than what he has provided for you. You're not a dog to be used and abused by his fucked up delusional power. You're a treasure. One that should be handled with the utmost care and respect. You deserve the world, Esme, not just the slice of hell he's tried to shackle you down with. You deserve everything…"

My words hung heavy between us as she silently wept and I laid every emotion I had for her on the line. I stared at her trembling lips, desperate to kiss away any fragile feelings plaguing her.

"Emilio," she whispered, cupping my face with her slender hand.

"Yes, Esme?"

This was it. I could feel it in my bones. I'd finally did the impossible and melted the iceberg around her heart. My body inched closer as she brushed some stray strands of hair away from my face. Her vulnerability was alluring, and I was drawn to it like a beacon of light that burned radiating hope. I was finally going to get our wedded kiss, the kiss my body had craved since she ran away from me at the altar.

"Can you please pass the churros?" she asked, pulling away from me coldly.

And just like that, the radiating hope my body yearned for was a smoldering pile of ash, once again faced with the harsh reality that I'd never unthaw a heart made purely of ice.

Chapter Nine

Dear Abuelita,

Can you tell me what it's like to be truly loved? Is love worth all the heartache that comes with putting yourself out there, giving in to the raw emotion that threatens to rip you apart when you submit yourself to someone with a pure soul?

I almost let him kiss me. I felt his breath whisper across my lips, and it was like I could feel his soul reaching out for me at the same time mine reached for his.

He's too good for me, Abuelita. Emilio is the type of man that can provide a false sense of hope that there is true happiness in this world out there for all of us to catch. I don't even know what this emotion is that I'm feeling, but it's creating a havoc inside of me that I can't seem to shake.

I went to bed tonight touching my pussy as I envisioned him between my legs, bringing me to an orgasm on his molten hot tongue. In my mind, when he would kiss me, it tasted of cinnamon churros. Our tongues danced together in a forbidden salsa, weaving through the crevices of our mouths like trained professionals.

I felt it, Abuelita, that moment of piece and serenity. That slight ray of hope that seemed so far out of my reach. I was on the edge of a mind-blowing orgasm thinking about Emilio, but I never reached that peak... I never got that moment of release my body desperately craved.

A memory that I had locked away in the recesses of my mind, crashed through it like a wrecking ball, throwing me back to that fateful night when Julio first joined me in bed. I was almost eighteen. Emilio was gone and Sergio was doing everything he could to avoid me. Mateo was far too young for me to hang out with, so I was stuck inside, reading every book in Julio's library as I cried myself to sleep.

There was a quiet knock on my door and Julio stepped in, finding me on the bed crying into my pillow. His burly hands curled around my body, cradling me against his massive chest protectively.

"There, there. I'm here now. Don't cry, Esmeralda, you're too beautiful to cry."

"You think I'm beautiful?" I asked him, swallowing a sob that shook through my body.

His predatory gaze wandered over the slip that barely covered my small chest. I felt his hand running higher and higher up my thigh until it was resting between my legs, hovering a few inches away from my pussy. He started to stroke my leg, the intimate movement creating confusion inside of me.

On one hand, his embrace felt fatherly, like Padre was alive and there to soothe me. But the way his hand felt between my legs, had my senses going wild.

"I think you're the most beautiful creature I have ever seen."

No man had ever looked at me that way before, with eyes overruled by desire and a gaze that said he thought I was beautiful.

"Really?"

"Yes. I remember the night I brought you home. You were so broken and fragile. That was the night I fell in love with you, Esmeralda, the night I knew you would one day be mine."

"Yours?" I asked him.

"Yes… but I had to wait until you were of age. Now that you are, would you like me to show you how much I love you and why you are mine?"

"I do. Make me feel loved, Julio. Show me why I'm yours."

I was too young and broken to really fathom what I was encouraging. Nobody could possibly understand where I was in that moment. Do you see how fucked up my headspace was, Abuelita? Being treated like a hideous beast every time someone looks at you isn't easy. When I tried to hang out with Sergio—the man I was destined to marry someday, he looked at me in disgust, all because of the scar that was still healing repulsively on my face. He hated me because I was no longer a virgin bride, and I think he only fucked me because I was there. He never loved me… nobody ever loved me.

Hearing their father tell me I was beautiful and that he loved me was everything I needed to keep going. I was slightly dead inside before then, circling the drain of depression in a leaky boat without a paddle. It took his touch to breathe life back into me. Feeling those massive hands move from my thigh to under my panties was the best feeling in the world. I belonged to someone—I belonged to him. And in that moment, he had me believing every sick, fucked up word he said.

I can see through his lies now, Abuelita. He never loved me. He was just a predator that was searching for someone weak to take advantage of. I was an easy target, one that was wooed by his dedicated touch and quickly spewed lies. It took me this long to see it, Abuelita. That wasn't real love, that was him taking advantage of a naïve and broken girl, one that is still fractured and fighting to be put back together.

Why can't I picture Emilio making love to me without Julio's ugly face breaking up my thoughts? Has that man tainted my soul so much that I'll be forced to sleep in his bed forever, never knowing what love truly is?

I decided that tomorrow I'm going to experience everything I've never had a chance to before, taking Emilio up on his offer for me to make all the choices for our day.

Maybe if I distract myself with frivolous things, I'll be able to erase the memories that keep hounding me at night.

Julio taking advantage of me isn't the only memory that defiles my nightmares… the night I received my scar still haunts me to this day. That night my innocence was claimed by a man in a ski mask, stealing it away from whatever man I married.

But it's four in the morning and I need to try to sleep, so I'll save that memory for another day.

Until tomorrow, Abuelita. I hope you are smiling down on me from heaven with my parents and brothers by your side. I miss you all.

Siempre te amaré,

Esme

Chapter Ten

I read her latest journal entry while she was taking a shower. The vehement rage that coursed through my body when I read what that bastard did to her, had my hands curling, ready to punch the first thing that got in my way.

My father had always been a shitty person, but for him to seduce and prey on Esme when she was at her weakest, broke my heart in two. Now I knew why he kept sending me away for my summers. Sergio wanted nothing to do with her at the time, and my father could see that my feelings for her went far beyond the friendship we shared.

He had me redirect those feelings into Louisa the first summer, and the second I spent with my abuelita, mourning over her death. It was a skilled play; a chess move that had me cornered with barely any moves to get out. I fell for it— his misdirection leading me into the bed of another woman—one that he would take away from me, too. Then leaving me to suffer with the pain of losing her.

Would things be different had I stayed home that second summer? Would it have been me in her bed instead of him? I grabbed a glass from off the kitchen counter and chucked it at the wall, getting a moment of satisfaction as it hit the tiles and shattered apart on impact.

That bastard would pay for everything he did to Esme and me. When we get back, I'll do everything I can to keep her from climbing back into his bed, even if it means tying her up in my own just so she can't retreat and leave me.

"I heard a crash, what happened?" she asked, eyeing the glass all over the floor and counter. She stood before me in nothing but a towel, her beautiful ebony hair hanging wet against her back.

I don't know what came over me in that moment, maybe it was my carnal need to protect her, but I stalked across the room, only stopping when I could scoop her into my arms and carry her back into the bedroom.

"Emilio, what the hell is wrong with you? What are you doing?" She smacked and hit my back, but I could barely feel it against my already numb body.

She didn't know I read her words, but I wasn't about to let her continue seeing my father's face in place of mine. The spell had to be broken and there was only one way of doing that… making love to my wife for the very first time.

Her back hit the mattress when I dropped her down, and she laid beneath me, breathing erratically as she stared at me with widened eyes. My gaze raked over every glorious inch of her. The towel had fallen off her body before we even crossed the threshold of the bedroom door.

This time she was sober and would remember every sweet kiss I placed on her.

"Stop," she called out in horror, placing her palms flat against my chest. "I can't do this."

With one quick movement, I had her arms pinned above her head, as the rest of her body curled around my torso.

"That's where you're wrong, Esme. You can do this. Your body and mind need this. Let me erase every man that ever came before me. Where their kisses have tainted you, I will lick away the memories, replacing them with better ones that worship and devour you. Any polluted word ever spewed by a man to get you into their beds will be gone when I'm done with you. Please, let me do this. Let me make love to you."

She stared at me in silence, tears welling up in those caramel eyes, refusing to be shed. She was so utterly broken, and in desperate need of someone to piece her back together.

"Are you asking me, or telling me?" she questioned, motioning with her head to my dominant move that had her pinned beneath me.

"I told you yesterday that this day was all about you making choices. Yes, I may have carted you off like a caveman and carried you to bed, but I won't kiss or touch you unless you tell me it's okay. All I want is to show you the love that burns inside of me every time I look into your eyes. It's the same love that creates impossible heart beats that thump inside my chest when you walk in the room. If you tell me to get off you, I will. If you ask me to leave, I'll find a place on the beach and sleep under the stars in the chill of the night. But if you let me in, I promise you that everything will change. You won't belong to him anymore; you'll belong to me. Right where you've always belonged."

One stray tear dripped from her left eye. It was like a scarf dropping in the middle of a street race. The second it disappeared over her chin, she said, "Then it's my choice to let you in. Make love to me, Emilio. Show me who I truly belong to."

Chapter Eleven

My thumb gently traced the outside of her scar as my gaze dropped to her plump lips. Without a second thought, I dipped down, brushing my mouth over hers, inhaling her slight gasp as the electricity within that kiss sparked to life.

I went super slow, taking my time with her. Letting her open to me before taking my tongue into her hot mouth and rolling it inside. Letting go of her hands, my tender touch tickled down her front, brushing over the tops of her aroused nipples and down her torso, feeling every rib on her malnourished body, and the goosebumps that came to life as my fingertips brushed even further down her cooled skin.

Remembering everything Juliet and Louisa taught me, my mouth followed the same path as my fingertips, nipping at every curve on her body until I was between her legs, my mouth hovering over the small tuft of hair that pointed to her pussy.

"You're so fucking beautiful," I gasped, sealing my words with a sweet kiss to the most intimate part of her body. Her whole body arced into me, a slight gasp escaping her lips as I pressed my mouth to her center. Teasing her with my tongue, I elicited desperate squirms that took over her, creating chaos as I brought her pleasure.

"Please," she begged.

"What, Esme? What are you asking for?"

I knew what she wanted. Her whole body was singing in anticipation, reacting to every slow stroke of my tongue, and thrust of my finger that brought her pleasure.

"Make me cum," she hissed out, wiggling beneath me as my fingers curled upward and hit her from the back. "Oh, my God," she screamed as my tongue swirled in a new direction, repeating slow methodical circles that hit every nerve in her body. Her first orgasm came suddenly, her walls becoming slick with her cum as she moaned in utter disbelief.

She was super sensitive to my actions, creating endless quaking that rippled through her body. Her painted nails curled into the sheets beneath her, legs squeezing my head as she fought the second orgasm that gripped her unexpectedly.

When I pulled my mouth away, she shot up, her eyes dancing with a frustrated need that looked primal. She grabbed my shorts, quickly undoing the belt and removing my clothing until I was as naked as she was.

Her mouth engulfed my hard cock, immediately taking it to the back of her throat, swallowing every inch until it was buried inside her. My balls tensed as she hungrily sucked my dick. There was an anxiousness about each bob of her mouth, and I gripped her hair, guiding her head along my shaft as she milked me for seed. She almost had me there, but I didn't want to cum the first time in her mouth, I wanted it to be in her pussy, deep inside that forbidden part of her that she'd never given me before.

"Hold on, baby. When I cum for the first time in you, it will be deep inside your womb." I gently tipped up her chin, guiding her to her knees, so that she was within kissing distance. My hands wrapped around her torso, pulling her close as my mouth met hers, kissing her so delicately that you could feel the passion vibrating inside your bones.

She moaned against my mouth as I gently circled her clit with my hands, diving into the wet slit as I continued making love to her mouth.

She pulled away from me, getting on all fours, displaying her backside to me.

"No, no, Esme. We aren't fucking tonight. We're making love." My hands gripped her hair, pulling her back until she was flush against my chest. I leaned back on my knees, angling her until she was sliding down my cock in my favorite reverse cowgirl position. The whole time I clutched her body, keeping our frames as close as possible, as my mouth found hers and I stroked in and out of her.

"Holy shit!" she moaned into my mouth.

It was an awkward position for most, but I knew how to fenagle it, so it pleasured both of us. We started slow, picking up speed until her moans broke our kisses, and she was completely consumed by our union.

In a swift jerk, I was out of her, placing her on her back so that she was looking up at me as I eased into her once again, lifting her leg for the deepest penetration.

"I love you, Esme, I've always loved you. I know you'll probably never love me back, but every time you open yourself up to me this way, you will feel the love I feel toward you, burning inside. My love for you is like a forest fire that rages out of control. The slightest spark ignites another flame, ensuing chaos as it burns a path of destruction."

She briefly opened her eyes that were pinched together in ecstasy. There were so many questions lost in them, but the one I could see the most was the one that had her questioning whether she felt the same.

I pressed a single finger to her lips, shushing whatever word she felt forced to say in that moment. "Shush, you don't have to say a word. Falling in love takes time, and I'm determined to catch you as you plummet down from the pedestal I've placed you on, right into my awaiting arms. When you're ready, that four letter word will topple from these succulent lips, and you'll know in your heart that you mean every letter attached to it. I know we need time to grow with each other, and I'm ready to wait an eternity to win your heart. You're a race worth entering, and I'll keep going until I've scored the ultimate prize— you. For now, just give in to the way our bodies meld perfectly together. I want you to feel every stroke deep inside your soul, paying attention to how our hearts beat to the same rhythmic melody as our moving bodies. Because this is making love, Esmeralda, and if you've never experienced this before, then you've never been loved by a man who thinks you're the center of their world like I do. I may not have the power of my father, or the strength and aim of my brother, but I am a man who loves with every ounce of his soul, Esme, and that soul belongs to you—it's belonged to you since the day you came to live with us. I'm yours… forever, now, and always."

She didn't answer me with anything but her screams as she reached the pinnacle orgasm, one that rocked through her whole body. It was the same orgasm that had me spilling my seed in her for the very first time. She may have the devil living inside her sometimes, but the way my soul burned for this woman was a purgatory I'd never forget.

This union ruined me for all others. I'll never look at another woman the way I look at Esme. She was a wounded deer that I was determined to nurse back to health, and if she let me love her, I'd show her just what it was like to be cherished and appreciated for being beautiful. There wasn't a scar on this planet that could make me see her any differently. She was beautiful, and in that moment, she was finally something else too… mine.

Chapter Twelve

Dear Abuelita,

If you saw any of that from heaven, I apologize. What happened in that bedroom was beyond mind-blowing. Emilio had my body peaked and spiraling over the edge with even the slightest touch.

He was right. I've never had a man make love to me before—not like that. That fire he spoke about, I could feel it burning inside of me. It was like he waas a match and I was the burning flame dancing down the splintering piece of wood.

I'm still trying to come down off the high being with him has brought to me. Giving myself over to Emilio was the hardest thing I ever had to do. He completely ruined me for all other men. I'll never look at sex and intimacy in the same way again. I'd always viewed it as a weapon, something men used to control women, or women used to control men.

I've tried to think back to every sexual experience I've ever had, searching for a moment that even remotely holds up to this one. None can touch it. It was like Emilio knew exactly everything to say and do to keep me going. We've barely left the bedroom, taking every opportunity to make love to each other.

Right now, his love holds us together, and I can already feel emotions starting to form deep inside of me. That wall I built up around my heart is being dismantled brick by painful brick.

I was once told, that in order to love someone, you have to let go of your past… I've decided that it's time for my husband to know everything about me —even that horrific night that still loops in my nightmares.

Telling him is the only way I can truly let him in… but will he see me differently after he experiences the worst part of me—the part of me that sits permanently broken and guarded?

I have to try, Abuelita. I have to give in to these feelings he's creating inside me. I just hope he will forgive me for the secrets I'm about to share. Once he finds out, there's no telling what he'll do.

He's like a festering storm, waiting for something to spin him violently out of control. He may know all the right moves in the bedroom, but is he man enough to stand up to the monsters who turned me into the cold-hearted woman I am today? Will he still love me when he takes me apart and sees the unfinished pieces scattered inside me?

I will not stop, Abuelita, not until every ounce of their blood has been spilled. They're like the fucking hydra. Once one head is cut off, another three pop up. I can't count how many there have been, but once I find the heart of the monster, I will pierce daddy's dagger into it, stealing every beat until all the monsters who killed our family are beheaded, and the never-ending beast has been slain.

That's how revenge works. Revenge is something that I know like it's a part of me. It's love that still remains a mystery to me. But Emilio is determined to help me find it, and his advances have weakened me emotionally.

He found that small crack in my defenses, and now I'm powerless against him. He used a weapon I didn't know how to defend myself against, and now I'm a victim to his words as much as I am to his kisses. That man breathes passion like he was born inhaling it, and I can't help but find myself wanting him to pass the joint, allowing me to inhale the toxic fumes that seem to be his driving force.

I need something to drive me—something other than a bitter heart that's thirsting for blood.

Pray for me, Abuelita. Let's see how much he still loves me after he finds out that I murder men in cold blood, ridding the world of their filthy destruction and the cocks that defiled me when I was too young and weak to defend myself.

If he can still love me after that, then I will never return to his father's bed again. Not when I have someone that loves every part of me, even the part I try to hide and keep secret from everyone else around me.

Siempre te amaré,

Esme

Chapter Thirteen

Esme never spoke to me after she wrote that journal entry. I waited, hoping she would open up to me, but she never did. Instead, I spent the rest of our honeymoon showering her with love, doting on her every whim, creating smiles that were genuine and filled with pure glee. For those few glorious days, we lived in wedded bliss, enjoying each other's company, exploring each other in every way possible.

Her journal entry haunted me. Reading the words on those pages, knowing her hands were coated in metaphorical blood, it does something to you. Did I fear her? No. Did I understand why she chose that path? Absolutely not. But I decided to love her despite her shady past. We could get through it—we could get through anything if she was open to experiencing it together.

We could even stand up to my father. I knew that strength existed in both of us, but Esme seemed to run on two things... fear and vengeance.

She gripped my hand tightly as we stood outside the awaiting plane that was ready to take us home back to Mexico, to all those demons she was desperately trying to run away from.

Tears formed in her eyes. Turning to me, she sniffed, wiping away a few stray tears that danced down her cheeks.

"I can't go back, Emilio. Not to him. Not to that house..." She took a shuddering breath, trying to calm the anxiety plaguing her. "He's going to want me again. He believes I'm his."

"And are you?" I asked, taking a step forward, sweeping her hair away from her face so I could look into her eyes that reminded me of a baby fawn and warm caramel.

"I used to think so," she whispered, her eyes migrating to the dusty floor of the hangar. "I thought that walking alongside the

Capo of the Santoyo Cartel would help me…" her voice trailed off, leaving me hanging like her last journal entry.

"Help you what?"

She looked up at me, her eyes shimmering with so much pain and self-deprecation. You could see the damnation in those eyes, how she created a prison that had her mind cornered and trapped in her own personal hell.

"Help me kill those bastards who disfigured me and killed my family. I want them all fucking dead, every goddamn one of them. But he never helped me… I had to do everything myself. The blood on my hands would taint you, Emilio. You're so sweet and sensitive, and I'm a cold-blooded murderer. You should've never been forced to marry someone as horrific as me. I'm a monster… not only on the outside, but inside as well."

Hearing the words tumble out of her lips was like stepping on a thousand tiny thumbtacks, pricking me hard and imbedding in my heart, refusing to move.

She stomped away from me, dropping into a seat near a wall. Immediately, her head was slumped forward, and she hung her head heavily in her hands.

The pilot told us it would be another hour before the plane would take off. He was doing his system checks. There was no one but us in the small hangar, and I knew that it was time for my wife to release the demons she held onto so dearly.

"Hey," I whispered, dropping to my knees in front of her. Lifting her chin, I forced her to look me in the eye, hating the mix of emotions I saw raging in her frustrated gaze. "You're not a monster, Esme. You're a woman who was tortured and abused. Even the sweetest animal can turn on their owners if forced into a corner. I'm not saying you're an animal, but I am saying that you had every right to defend yourself if you felt you had no other choice. Tell me about that night… the night my father brought you home in the rain."

Esme took a deep breath, the life in her eyes draining away as she mentally thought back to what was probably the most traumatic thing she ever had to go through.

"You won't look at me the same way after I tell you the story, Emilio."

"Try me…"

"It's a graphic story, not something for those with weak hearts. If you can't stomach the dark shit, then my story will haunt you for an eternity."

"I can handle it, Esme. I want to know everything about you, even the things you wish you could lock away to never resurface again."

She nodded weakly, taking my hand so she could grip it tightly. "I can't do details, they hurt too much. But I can give you the basics."

"Okay," I replied, giving her an encouraging smile.

"It was late. My father had just returned from an important business meeting with your father. I believe they were discussing my future because when he came home, he gave me the guiltiest look in the world, like he just sold my soul to the devil or something. I heard him and my mother arguing in the bedroom about me. My father kept repeating I was too young, while my mother simply stated it was what was best for the familia. I remember her saying that there were worse things that could happen to me than being married to a Santoyo man. My father's voice got even louder after she said that, simply stating, *says the bitch who keeps fucking one.*"

My eyes widened and Esme must've seen my surprise.

"Yeah, that's right. Your father was fucking my mother on the side. Just another side piece for him to get his dick wet in." She rolled her eyes. "Your father is an asshole, but he has a way of wooing women into his bed. Somehow, he convinced my mother to join him there, corrupting her just like he corrupted me. It's why my bitch of a mother slapped my father that night. She did it fucking hard, too. I could hear it all the way down the hall from where I was hiding. My father never hit her back, he just stood their stoically, looking at her with shame and hidden rage. He told her that it would be over his dead body that I'd ever marry a Santoyo man—especially not Julio. My guess is that your father approached him about me marrying him, and my father said fuck no, then he tried to strong arm him into arranging something between me and Sergio. After that, they went to sleep in their separate rooms, keeping their distance from each other. Nothing happened for a few days, then my father got into an altercation with a few men on the street. He got roughed up pretty bad. He said they were from the Ramirez Cartel. You can always tell if someone is part of that cartel by…"

"The rose on their forearms," I finished for her.

She nodded. "They broke four of my father's ribs and gave him matching black eyes. When he came home that night, he was barely walking. I heard him call your father and ask for his help, begging him to retaliate before the Ramirez's struck again. But your father said no, told my father that unless he gave into his demands, he wasn't doing shit to help our familia. My father was so scared, I've never seen him that frightened before. He barely could hold up his glass of whiskey as he tried to gulp it down. It was almost as if he knew that death was on the horizon. That's the night I woke up to screaming. When I came out to see what was going on, I saw my mother being dragged out of her bedroom by huge masked men. There were about twenty men in my house, all of them dressed in black from head to toe, and the only thing you could see was their eyes poking out of their ski masks. I felt someone grab me from behind, and I started kicking and screaming as they carried me to the living room where my father, mother, and two younger brothers were being held at gunpoint on the floor. I can't tell you anymore. The rest of it I've tried to block out."

"I understand, you only have to tell me what you want to, Esme."

She blinked away a tear, her entire body going rigid from the memory. "I still feel their hands sometimes. I don't think I'll ever be able to forget the pure brutality they inflicted on me and my family. The parts I do remember I will never forget, like watching that masked man take the lives of every member of my family. The terror in my father's eyes as he had to watch…" she trailed off again and swallowed before speaking. "He started with my mother, then my brothers, finally stopping briefly with my father. He held the gun to his temple as he whispered something in his ear. Then my father's pained eyes met mine for the last time. BOOM! After that, all I remember is waking up in the gutter of a cold, wet alley barely alive. Julio somehow found me and saved my life. Maybe if he had just come to my aide quicker, none of that bloodshed would've happened and my familia would still be here today."

I embraced her, squeezing her with all the might in my body, wishing I could erase that painful memory.

She pulled away from me, her eyes practically trembling with unshed tears. "I saw the tattoos on their forearms. All the men there that night had that same damn rose tattoo… and I told myself I wouldn't stop until every man from that fucking crime family was dead. Any life I have taken has been in vengeance for my family but picking them apart hasn't been easy. I have to take them out one by one, making sure nobody puts two and two together. But I will tell you one thing, every member of the Ramirez Cartel that I have killed was left pleading for their lives, just like they left my familia pleading for theirs. I started at the bottom and I'm working my way through their ranks. Until I find that man who took everything away from me. I'm gonna kill him, and once I do, I'm going to dance in his blood and bathe in it. After that, maybe I'll finally be free of all these damn pesky demons that won't leave me the hell alone." She looked up at me in defeat. "Go ahead, you can say it. I'm a fucking monster."

"You're not a monster, Esme. You're an avenging angel. I may not have blood on my hands like you do, but that doesn't mean I can't see why you did what you had to. I grew up in this life, I've watched men die for less. If anything, I think more of you for being able to stand up to those who harmed you. I wish I was that brave. Maybe if I was, I wouldn't be so scared to return home and face him again."

Esme cupped my face, forcing me to look her in the eyes. "You are brave, Emilio. You're also kind, and good-natured. You don't belong in this world."

"Esme, I belong in whatever world you exist in." I sealed my words with a kiss, feeling the anxiety both of us felt about returning to my father's home through our lips. It was like we quaked together, one massive jumble of limbs connected by a single common thread—the fear of Julio Santoyo and his wrath that was destined to affect us both. What exactly would we be walking into when we got back? Would I be able to stand up to him and keep his filthy paws off my wife?

Those were the questions running through my mind as the pilot shuffled us onto the plane. They lingered there the entire flight, and just before the wheels touched down on the tarmac of our home airport, I turned to Esme and said… "Let's run away together."

Chapter Fourteen

In a perfect world, our plan to run off like my brother would've worked. We'd be somewhere on an island far away, far from the clutches of my father and the familia. But like always, life was a giant cock fucking me in the ass.

The second we stepped off the plane, I saw him. There was no hiding—no running away. Not when Julio Santoyo himself was standing next to a car parked two feet from the airplane. He was surrounded by five of his best men, all of them waiting on us.

"There he is!" my father bellowed; a strange unwelcomed happiness laced in his words. He spoke those three words like he was excited to see me, but that could only mean one thing… he wanted something, something that brought him out of the safety of his compound and straight to the airport to pick us up.

Esme clutched my hand, tiny shivers quivering through her tiny frame. She immediately hid behind her hair, shielding her scar from my father's line of vision. It was what she always did whenever she was out in public, making sure her massive black locks concealed the one part of her she was afraid of people seeing.

"Padre?" I questioned carefully. "Why are you here?"

"Can't a man pick up his son and beautiful wife from the airport. So, how was it? Did you love the Bahamas?" A strange smile formed across his usually scowling face.

"They were beautiful. Thank you for paying for the trip," I cautiously replied.

My father's massive hand hit my shoulder, causing pain that instantly radiated down my forearm. He didn't do it to hurt me, he legit wanted to congratulate me on marrying Esme. Who was this man? Why was he being overly nice to me for no reason?

"Did you fuck her and break in that married pussy?"

"I don't think that's any of your business," I coldly stated, pulling out of his grasp.

My father's smile faltered for a half a breath, then returned like what I said didn't piss him off. "You did!" his eyes danced in delight. "Hear that, boys? Emilio actually got her to fuck him." He laughed, gripping my shoulders even tighter. "Didn't think she'd let ya, but like always, you worked your magic on her." He turned to Esme. "Did my son fuck you good?"

"Better than you," she quietly mumbled, only loud enough for me to hear.

"What the fuck did you just say?"

"I said, only because he had to." She darted a look my way, showing me with her eyes that she was lying to save the both of us.

"Good. Good. Now that you're back, we have some business to tend to, Mijo. I've called Mateo, he's on his way to meet us at the house. There's a family meeting we need to have, and I want you both to be there. Esme, when you get back to the house, I want you to unpack and then be ready for me when I'm done with my meeting. He echado de menos a mi perra." **I have missed my bitch.**

My fingers curled by my side, every courageous bone in my body solidified all at once. "She's not returning to your bed. And don't call her a fucking bitch. My wife deserves respect, not to be treated like a damn dog!"

I wanted to stop the words as soon as they left my mouth. The crease in my father's forehead bowed with his narrowed eyes, mouth ticking up in a ferocious scowl. Then, a few seconds later, it disappeared, replaced with that fake smile again.

"HA! My son grew some balls while in the Bahamas. Good. Good. You're going to need them for what comes next."

He opened the car door and Esme climbed inside, I started to follow her in, but I felt my father's fingers digging into the back of my neck, holding me back. His moustache tickled my ear as he leaned in and said. "You can have your fun with her for now, but when I want her, I will fucking take her. She may be your wife, but she fucking belongs to me. Defy me again, and I'll put a bullet in the back of your skull."

Then he kissed my cheek, pretending like he didn't just threaten to take my wife and kill me.

Esme held my hand the whole way home, her fingers digging into my skin. She was trying not to cry. Within minutes, my father had broken her again. It was a gift it seemed—the ability to tear apart a person with only poisonous words.

When we arrived at the house, Mateo was already there, sitting on the living room couch looking exhausted. A few weeks ago, my father put me with the daunting task of following my littlest brother around. He was like a stealthy ninja, always evading me when he found me stalking him. It took me almost a week to figure out what he was doing, but I never told my father once I did. No. Some things are better left unsaid. What Mateo was doing could get him killed. Insubordination was something our father didn't tolerate, and if I told him that Mateo was running his own black-market business stealing expensive artifacts and paintings, he'd kill him, not thinking twice about it. I must admit, Mateo's cat burglar skills were evolutionary! One night I witnessed him breaking into a house, stealing a painting, all before the alarms ever noted he was there. He definitely had a talent for going unnoticed, something he had strived for in the familia for years.

"Good, you're here. Esme, get the fuck upstairs, my boys and I have business to tend to."

Esme quickly disappeared, leaving me alone with my brother and father.

"Padre, what is this all about?"

"Well, now that your brother has decided to betray the family, I've decided it's time to announce my next in line. You, Emilio, you're going to be the next Capo of this familia."

My heart sped up in my chest. Being head of the familia was something I always desired, but now that I had Esme, the last thing I wanted to do was have anything to do with my father or his business.

"I'm getting older, and I'm not going to be around forever. Someone has to take over the business when I'm gone, and since the only son capable of running it betrayed me, that responsibility will now fall on your shoulders, Emilio. We all know it's what you wanted for a long time."

It was true. Before Sergio left, I was all about severing my father's devotion to him and taking his place as next in line. But after finding out all the shit my father did to Esme, and the corruption that surrounds this family, I don't want to do anything but take Esmeralda away from here and never look back.

"Why the fuck did you call me here?" Mateo asked, his jaw ticking with rage.

"You are a Santoyo son, are you not?"

"Debatable."

The second the word left his lips; my father's hand was smacking Mateo across the face. "You're lucky your skills are useful to me, Mateo, or I'd be putting a bullet between those treacherous eyes."

"You already tried to put a bullet in me once, Old Man, why don't you take your shot and end my life now? We both know you've wanted to do that since the day I was born."

Our father stared at Mateo, disregarding his words before turning to me. "We have a phone call to make," he said abruptly, pulling out his cell phone. He dialed a number, then put his phone on speaker. The line picked up, but the person on the other side didn't say a word.

"I am in need of your services, but in a particular way. I have a job for you, Mr. X."

My blood ran cold. Hearing the notorious name out loud already had me quaking in my boots. My brother was good at his job—really good, but this man on the other line, the one only known as Mr. X, well, his reputation put my brother's to shame.

"I am listening," the distorted voice said.

"I have a problem that needs to be dealt with. It seems one of my sons has decided to leave the family. I can't have that. I need him and the bitch he ran off with back here. You can rough them both up, I don't care, but I need them alive. Can you do that?"

"That's not what I usually do," the voice replied.

"Can you do it for say half a million dollars?"

The man on the other line was eerily quiet. Then after a few agonizing minutes, he said, "Half a million per person. Less if you don't mind them coming back in body bags."

My father swore quietly under his breath. "One million it is. I need them both alive. How you get them here is up to you, but they need to be alive. I have plans for them both. Do that and the million is yours."

"Consider it done. Email me any information you have."

"Mr. X, before you go, I think I should warn you that this won't be easy. My son, he is the one that is known as El Planchazo, he won't go down without a fight."

The robotic chuckle that followed was almost comical. "Then your price just went up. One million for him and five hundred thousand for her."

My father's fingers tightened around the phone. That money meant nothing to him. He could wipe his ass with it, and it wouldn't touch our finances. Our cartel brought in hundreds of thousands daily. My father made that much in a week. But like any proud man, money was power to my father, and giving that power over to someone else wasn't in the cards for him. His jaw tensed as he gritted out, "Done."

"Then we have a deal. Don't contact me again. I'll contact you." The line went immediately dead.

My father smiled deviously. "It won't be long until I have all my sons again. Mateo, I want you to track your brother, find out where that motherfucker is hiding and send me the information, Mr. X will do the rest."

"If he's so notorious, then why am I doing the grunt work for him?"

He didn't even flinch when my father's hand whipped his face to the side. "Shut your fucking mouth, Mateo. I'm sick of you always running your goddamn mouth with me. As Capo of this organization, you should show me the damn respect I deserve."

"Respect is earned, not beat into people. If you wanted my respect, you should've figured out a way to treat me better— maybe even love me and shit."

My father's silence wasn't a good thing. It meant he was on the cusp of erupting. His rage mirrored an angry volcano set out to destroy the world with festering ash. Just like a poisonous snake, my father's bite mirrored an African bush viper. Mean, painful, and lacking the antivenin to come back from it.

"Love? LOVE! Why the fuck would I ever love a worthless piece of shit like you? Hell, I barely love Emilio and Sergio. The only person I have ever loved, betrayed me and is now dead. If you want love, go find yourself some whiny bitch and get to fucking. Now find me fucking Sergio and get the fuck out of my sight, you've successfully fucked up my mood."

Mateo immediately jumped up, ready to stalk from the room. He had only made it two feet when my father grabbed a metal sculpture from off the wall and cracked it over Mateo's head, knocking him to the ground.

"Padre!" I yelled, moving to pick Mateo up off the floor.

"Don't touch him. If he wants to leave the room without addressing me, then he can crawl along the floor with the rest of the bottom feeders."

Mateo didn't cry or lash out. No. He struggled to get to his feet, only to be kicked in the ribs. This happened three more times before he literally had to crawl across the floor like a worm.

Tears pricked my eyes. I felt for my brother, but I was so helpless. I couldn't take a beating like that. I'd be dead. So, I just stood there quietly, dying on the inside for being so weak and unable to help my brother.

Once he was gone from the room, my father turned to me. "Follow me, Emilio, we have some serious issues to discuss."

I sulked behind my father, biting all the words that threatened to tumble out of my mouth. My weakness was showing and the lack of backbone I had when it came to my father was creating confliction inside my heart. If I couldn't stand up for my brothers, how the hell am I going to stand up to him when it comes to my own wife?

Chapter Fifteen

Sometimes reality smacks you in the face when you least expect it. I fell in love in the Bahamas. In love with the idea of being with someone who loved me so deeply, he would do anything to bring me happiness, even run away to escape all my demons. In love with the world he created for me—a world without Julio Santoyo and his violent tendencies. In love with falling in love and opening myself up to someone who doesn't look at me like I'm a monster.

The bitch slap I felt when we touched down in Mexico was the cold reality hitting me hard. Everything had definitely not changed, and it crippled me. There was a small moment where I actually believed we could make it, where I could live with Emilio somewhere else and not have to feel Julio breathing down our necks.

Then he was there, staring at us with a pathetic painted on smile, undressing me with his gaze while beating me down like a stray dog at the same time.

Even though Emilio held my hand, and his strength calmed me, I knew nothing changed. I'd be back in Julio's bed by the end of the week. He'd drag me there kicking and screaming if he had to. He wasn't a man that just let people exist in happiness. He has to corrupt it—taint it, filling it with his venomous poison and lies.

After Emilio's conversation with his father, something changed. Emilio was so cold to me. He came into his bedroom wearing a significant black eye. His lip was busted, and there was a scrape along his cheek that wasn't there before. When I asked what happened, he walked straight into his bathroom and locked the door. I swear I heard him crying behind the barrier that separated us. His silent sobs may have been muffled by the splintered wood, but I could still hear them—maybe even feel them in my soul. Whatever Julio said, broke Emilio. He can't look at me without tears forming in his eyes. He doesn't shed a single one, but the strength he had in the Bahamas is gone. He's cowering again, slinking around and falling in step behind Julio like a dutiful son.

When we laid down next to each other that night in bed, he stared at the ceiling, his fists clenching the sheets as he fought the urge to hold me. Anytime I opened my mouth to talk to him, he would turn over, refusing to look at me.

I don't know what I did wrong, Abuelita. How could he go from loving me to hating me within an hour? Maybe tomorrow he will tell me what happened, but for now, while he takes a shower and I sit here naked in the bed, scribbling my thoughts to you, so cold and alone, I'll just let my degrading thoughts break me down further, ripping me apart like everything else in my life.

It looks like Julio has won again, Abuelita. There's no defeating him. If I didn't need him to win my war against the Ramirez Cartel, he'd already be dead. I'd put the bullet in his head, woofing over him like the disobedient bitch he thinks I am.

But that's the sad part about life, Abuelita. Those who don't deserve to live, thrive like kings, and people like you, Papa, Mama, and my brothers are up there in heaven, watching as the villains of the world dismantle everything around them, creating destruction wherever they go.

Anyway, I just heard the shower go off. Until next time, Abuelita.

Siempre te amaré,

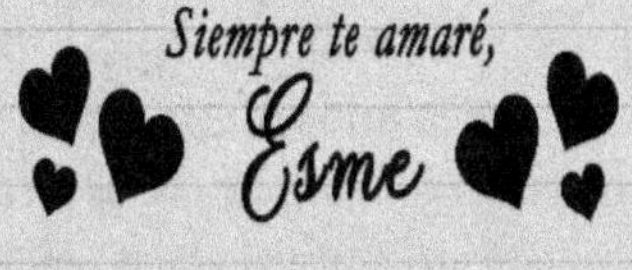

Chapter Sixteen

The guilt I felt after reading her latest journal entry was nothing compared to the turmoil and frustration raging a war inside me. I did ignore her and turn off my feelings, but it wasn't because of her, it was because of him—for breaking me—for revealing what he did.

That conversation was playing on a constant loop in my mind, revealing the sick and twisted things he did just to gain his power. I always knew he was a monster, but I never thought he was capable of doing what he did.

I gripped the bathroom sink, staring at the two massive black eyes he gave me and the split that separated the flesh of my lip. The one time I decide to stand up to him—the one time it mattered more than anything else, he beat me down, using his fists to pummel me back into submission. He couldn't kill me. No, that would've been too fucking easy. He needed me now. I was a fucking rook in his manipulative game of chess; only moving along the path he placed me on. Always forward or backward, sometimes side to side, but never deviating from his methodical plan—one he's had since the day he brought her home.

"Padre, what is this about?" I asked him when he ushered me into his office and closed the door behind us. I was still fuming over what he did to Mateo, but I had no idea the worst was yet to come.

"Sit down, Mijo. I have a story to tell you."

"Story?"

I cautiously took a seat in front of him as he plopped down into his desk chair.

He steepled his fingers against his lips and gave me a wide smile. "There are many things you don't know about this organization, things that I've done to keep us on top and the Santoyo name bitter on people's tongues. The Santoyo name instills fear in everyone who hears it. You don't cross the Santoyos, if you do, you end up dead."

"You say this like it's stuff I didn't already know. I know you have killed people to get to the top. Sergio is the one who does most of your dirty work."

"And when I find him and that fucking bitch he ran off with, I'm going to make him pay for double-crossing me. But right now, that's not what's important. What's important is what you can do for me, Mijo."

"Me?"

"Yes, Emilio, you. You're the only one that can help me finish what I started years ago."

"I don't understand."

"Well, if you'd shut up for two minutes, maybe I can tell you."

Sitting back in the chair, I waved my hand, encouraging him to continue.

"Sometimes our greatest enemies are the ones that are closest to us, Mijo. Living this life has created a giant target on my back. I have to be careful who I do business with and who I don't. I don't have many allies, and the ones I do, have been strong-armed into that position. You can't really call anyone a friend in this business, nobody is really your friend—they want to be around you for the power you hold and all the wealth you possess. I only had one person I called a friend, and that was Esmeralda's father. He was like a brother to me, and I trusted him with my life. Then he betrayed my trust, and I vowed that I would do everything in my power to make that man suffer for what he did."

"What the hell did he do?"

"He stole from me. Tried to get his own side hustle going. That's how the Barrios Cartel was created. He took what we had built together and branched out, creating his own network of drug running. Within months, their cartel was rivaling ours, all

because that bastard chose to go behind my back and create his own empire. I fucking built him! That bastard wouldn't have had a fucking dime if it wasn't for me. So, for every dime he stole out of my pocket, I took it in other ways."

My gut started to churn, I could see where this was heading, and I wasn't liking what I was hearing. Digging my fingers into the wooden arm of the chair, I latched on, hoping that what he was about to say wasn't the nightmare I was already seeing inside my head. If it was, there's no telling what I'd do to him.

"It started with his wife. She was easy to hook. The bitch enjoyed getting fucked in the ass, something her bullshit husband refused to do. For months I fucked his whore of a wife, picturing your mother's face every time I shoved my cock in her tight pussy. She was good in the sack, easy on the eyes, but she would never have the beauty your mother had. Now Esmeralda, that was a different story. I watched her grow up into a very beautiful woman, and there were times when I looked at her that she reminded me of your mother. My adoration for her grew every day, and when Esmeralda's father found out that I was fucking his wife for over seven years, he changed his will, leaving everything to his only legitimate child, his daughter, Esmeralda. Those boys she had, those were my bastard children, tainted seeds I planted purposely within his familia. He wouldn't be able to look at them without seeing my damn face."

"So, you're telling me I have two other brothers, other than the two I already have?"

My father cocked his head and sneered. "Had, Mijo. Bastards are made bastards for a reason. Every fucking bastard child doesn't deserve to be on this goddamn planet." His hateful words had hidden meanings.

I had my theories. It was highly possible that Mateo was a bastard child, and that my mother had slept with someone else when she gave birth to him, but I didn't have proof other than his blue eyes and slightly lighter hair. He looked a lot like our mother from the pictures I saw, but his eyes were out of place in this family of darkness. It would explain why our father was so incredibly cruel to Mateo, why he was the one who was constantly beaten and abused. If he was a bastard, and this was my father's feelings about them, there was no reason for him to keep Mateo alive unless it was just another chess move in his fucked-up game of chess.

When I didn't reply to my father's comment, he continued. "Every time I looked at Esme, I saw your mother. The undeniable beauty—the sheer grace when she entered the room. It was like she was your mother, reincarnated. I needed her—I wanted her. So, I propositioned her father, asking him for his daughter's hand. He immediately told me no. He said that I already got his wife and sons, that he wasn't about to let me corrupt another person in his familia. That wasn't the answer I was looking for, but at that moment, I wasn't in a position to challenge him. So, I enacted a masterful plan, one that would bring the Barrios Cartel to their knees. At the time, I didn't know he had changed his will again, but I had his lawyer on payroll, and he fed me information. It specifically said I couldn't marry Esmeralda in his will, and that every dime in his estate would be left to her on her twenty-fourth birthday, should she survive him in death. His will never said one of my sons couldn't marry her, so I approached his wife about arranging a marriage between Esmeralda and my eldest son. She thought it was a great idea, maybe because I fed her false promises of her and I getting married after I killed her husband."

The entire time my father told his story, I stayed silent, quietly boiling on the inside, like a tea kettle ready to fucking explode. It was the one and only time I wished I had a gun on me. I was already calculating the perfect place to put a bullet in his forehead.

"He said no to that offer too, told me that it would be over his dead body before his daughter ever married a Santoyo man. Before he could change his will again, I hired some men to beat the shit out of him. They were ex-members of the Ramirez Cartel. A few of them liked to find side jobs, and bringing down the Barrios Cartel was something that interested every single one of

them—especially when I promised them generous compensation. They beat his ass, but the fucking asshole wouldn't submit. He went home, told his wife he was leaving her and the boys and taking Esmeralda with him. When she told me that, I had to act. I called up the men I hired and rehired them for a new job–eradicating Fernando Barrio and every member of his family from existence. I kept my men out of it, I didn't want it getting linked back to me, so I went alone, with nineteen former members of the Ramirez Cartel. We showed up in ski masks, ripping through their house, destroying everything we touched. It was fucking invigorating. They dragged every member of his family out of their beds and carried them into the living room where I waited—ready to strike. I'm sure you can guess what happened next," he said smugly.

I couldn't take it anymore. Launching myself over the desk, I grabbed my father by the throat, squeezing him as hard as I could, but I wasn't nearly strong enough, and he over-powered me quickly. My father kicked me hard, sending me sailing across the room and into his filing cabinet. He rubbed at his throat as he stalked toward me, grabbing me by the hair as he punched me three times, once in the mouth and twice in the eyes.

"You're going to fight your own father over that filthy bitch? I told you before, Emilio, women are fucking expendable. They're all cheating whores who are only good for two things, cleaning and fucking. Why waste your breath on such a hideous beast."

"She's not hideous! She's fucking beautiful, and you ruined her."

He smirked, holding me on the ground, pinning me with his arms and legs. "I did ruin her, and I sliced up her pretty little face so no man would ever want her again."

"Why? Why would you do that to someone so young—so vulnerable?"

"Because I couldn't let her walk around reminding me of your mother after I brought her home. The scar was a necessity for her to exist in our world. Now, everybody knows not to fuck

with the Santoyo Cartel, otherwise, you end up like the Barrios, with a bullet in the head, six feet under, or a gigantic scar across your face."

"Why would you shoot your own children? Don't you have a heart?"

"I lost my heart when your bitch of a mother broke it. Those kids were nothing more than a liability. I already had two sons to carry on the Santoyo name, I didn't need two more."

"Mateo is your son, too!" I screamed out, doing everything I could to fight my way out from beneath my father's punishing grasp.

"That's another little secret of mine, Emilio. Mateo is not my son, and the only reason he's still alive is because he has a greater purpose, one that I'm getting ready to exploit very soon." Hearing him confirm my suspicions was like adding gasoline to a fire. He was fucking insane! Goddamn insane.

"Why are you telling me all this? What makes you think I won't run straight to Esme and tell her everything you did?"

My father reached behind his back and pulled out his gun, digging it into my chin. "Because if you say a fucking word to her, I'll fucking give you a visual of what happened that night. My men have tripled since then. Imagine over a hundred men carving up your bitch, maybe even passing her around like a joint so everyone gets a ride. Do you want her to go through that again, Emilio? Do you want to put her through that hell? Then go ahead, tell her. Let her know what I did, but the second you open your goddamn mouth, it will be the last words you'll ever say, because I'll blow your fucking brains out and won't think twice about it. After I force you to watch me defile and murder your wife of course."

The internal struggle I had fighting the tears that threatened to flow out of me was maddening. I didn't know what to do. The monster had reared his ugly head, and even though I knew who he was, I knew I couldn't tell Esme, not without putting her life at risk.

"What the fuck do you want from me?"

"In a few days we will be celebrating Esme's twenty-fourth birthday. I want you to convince her to sign over her inheritance to you. When she does, I want you to give that money to me."

"You've created all of this terror and chaos for fucking money? Why?"

"Because money is the only thing a person can rely on in this world, and I'm determined to get back every dime I was owed."

"What happens if I say no?"

"Then I kill you and your dog." He pressed the gun even harder into my throat, cutting off my ability to breathe. *"Fuck with me, Emilio, and I'll end your miserable existence just like I did your little brothers. Don't think I won't kill again."*

"They were your own flesh and blood!" I screamed, dumbfounded that this sick fuck created my DNA. My father was beyond evil, and I could see every corrupted spec in his dark eyes. He took villain to a whole other level. It sickened me that he had a hand in creating me. Bile formed in my throat just thinking about it.

"Familia antes que sangre, Mijo. Family before blood."

I'd vomited a million times since that meeting with my father, picturing the torture my father put Esme through that night, and how he took the lives of two of his own sons without any remorse. If he would kill them, what would stop him from killing one of us? The ones he actually raised since we were babies. Poor Esme, if she only knew that the man she was searching for had been sleeping in her bed for the last few years. What would she do? Would she kill him? Would she throw herself off that cliff she was talking about in her journal? He fucking stole everything from her, continuing to manipulate her over the years, breaking her apart piece by piece. I can't believe I looked up to this man for so long. The only person who didn't deserve to live on this planet was him.

My blood was like molten lava swimming through my veins. I was thirsting for vengeance, both for me and Esme. I knew in that moment, as I stared at my pitiful, sad reflection, that there was no turning back. Something had to be done.

I grabbed my phone, punching in one of the few numbers I knew by heart.

"Yeah?" his voice said on the other line.

"I know you can get ahold of him. I know he fucking hates me and there's no way he wants to return here, but we need him, Mateo."

"What makes you think I know where he is?"

"Because you're a whiz with computers, a fucking stealthy ninja when it comes to sneaking around, and you're one of the few people in the family he gives a fuck about."

He scoffed, but I could tell he was smirking at the same time. The best thing to get Mateo going is to pump up his ego.

"Please, Mateo, we fucking need him for this to work."

"For what to work?"

"To pierce the heart of the monster and destroy the hydra once and for all," I told him, remembering Esmeralda's journal entry and using the reference.

"You're speaking Greek, Hermano. Speak in a language I fucking understand."

"I want to put a bullet in Padre's head and fucking feed him to the rats."

"Fuck..." he paused for a long second. "Count me the fuck in."

"Can you find him?"

"Yeah, give me two seconds to track his burner... FUCK!"

"What? What's wrong?"

"GPS says he's already here."

Chapter Seventeen

My heart sank. If Sergio was already here, that could only mean one thing… Mr. X was here, too.

I dropped my phone, immediately rushing out into the hallway. My body smacked into Esme's as she was coming out of the bathroom, and she looked up at me with so many damn questions in her eyes.

"Is everything alright?"

"God, I hope so," I breathed, knowing the longer she stalled me, the more likely I was to end up without a brother

"Anything I can do to help?" she asked, running a warm hand up my bicep. I stared into those swirling pools of caramel, getting lost in the beauty of them.

"Trust me."

"Trust you?"

"I have plans, Esme… for us, but I can't involve you in them. Not yet. If I do, it could be bad for you. I need you to stay here and trust that I can take care of this situation. I'm doing what I can to ensure your safety, and a life full of happiness for you."

"So, you ignore me for three whole days, then when you finally say a word to me, all you can say is trust you?"

She took a step backward, putting even more of a distance between us than my silence already had created. I could see the hurt in her eyes. She was used to men treating her like shit, and I wasn't helping the situation at all.

"Esme, you need to trust me. I love you. I love you with every beat of my heart, but in order for us to be together, there are things I need to do. Things I don't want your beautiful hands tied in. Please, trust me. Let me do this for us—for our future."

"You can do whatever you want, Emilio. It doesn't mean I'll be here when you get back. You had me fooled when you said you loved me before, I won't fall for it again. I saw the way you looked at me when you came back from that meeting! You looked at me like I was disgusting—like you were repulsed by me. I can't go through that anymore. I've already had too many men in my life do that to me, I'm not letting you or anyone else in ever again."

She started to stomp away, but I reached out and grabbed her, pulling her into my arms and cradling her angry sobs, smothering them with love and devotion. "Don't hate me, Esme. Please. There is so much you don't know, and until I figure out a way to fix the problem, your life is in danger."

"What do you mean?" she asked, pulling away from me.

"I..."

"Your father wants to see you... both of you... NOW!" Eduardo ordered, staring at me with a strange fear in his eyes. Two weeks ago, our father had put a bullet in Eduardo's leg. Now the man was limping everywhere he went, you could see the pain in his eyes. It haunted him like the fear clearly riding through his features.

"She's staying here," I demanded, not wanting to get her tangled up in anything my father was up to.

I never saw the other man come up behind us. He grabbed Esme by the arms and hoisted her over his back. She started punching him, while kicking and screaming at him to let her down, but he didn't. Then I felt the press of cold metal meet the back of my skull. Another one of my father's men slinked in behind me, strong arming me to follow Eduardo and Esme.

"He said to bring you to him, not what condition you had to be in when we do. You want to make waves? I'll make sure you arrive to him like a surfboard eaten by a Great White Shark. Don't fuck with me, Emilio." The Santoyo name basically was only good if you were Sergio or my father. Mateo and I always had been treated differently by our father and his men. Nobody respected me, not like they should, being one of his sons and next in line to take over the Cartel, like my father said.

"Get your fucking hands off me, I'm going."

They shoved us into a vehicle, driving us to one of the many warehouses my father owned. The particular one we pulled up in front of was a meat factory that was a smoke screen for our drug business. On the outside, it looked like your typical meat factory, but a few floors below there was a fully operational drug house where we cooked out cocaine.

"Inside," the man barked, pressing the gun between my shoulder blades.

As we walked through the open doors, a man, one I'd never seen before, came strolling out with a briefcase. He was in a crisp white business shirt with black slacks and wore thick, wide-rimmed, black glasses. My skin crawled when he looked my way and his mouth ticked up slightly. He tipped his hat to me, then disappeared into the parking lot.

"Who was that?" I asked the man behind me.

"Like I know, get in there."

They pushed us toward the meat locker, then opened the door, pushing both me and Esme inside. The putrid smell of animal carcasses filled my nostrils. It was a vast freezer, and on the many hooks were the butchered bodies of cows, sheep, and pigs. They swung as I weaved past them, heading toward the back of the locker—my father's interrogation room.

The second I opened the door to the secret room, my heart dropped. There was my father sitting in a chair facing two people tied to chairs in front of him. One male. One female.

"Oh look, it's the newlyweds! I'm so happy you could join us. Sergio, tell your brother hello."

I walked around the chairs where my brother was tied up. He was covered in bruises from head to toe and was breathing erratically. The pure hatred in his eyes pierced my soul. Next to him sat a woman, passed out, with not a bruise on her. It was obvious that Sergio put up a fight, but his girl, Catalina, I believe is her name, was left untouched.

"You just missed my good friend Mr. X. Look at the present he has brought us. Any minute now your other brother should be arriving, then we can get this party started. First things, first…" He motioned behind us and I watched in horror as two men grabbed Esme, tying her to a chair like my brother and his girl.

"What the fuck are you doing?" I screamed at him.

"What I have to in order to get what I want, Mijo. You have many weaknesses, but your love for her is the biggest one you have." He stood up, walking over to Esme whose eyes widened in fear. He caressed her face, then grabbed her shirt, ripping it until he could see the tops of her bare breasts, shirt barely hanging on by a few threads and buttons.

"Stop touching her!" I screamed.

With one quick movement, my father turned, pointing his pistol at my face. "I'd suggest you shut your mouth, Emilio. There are many things we need to discuss, but not before your other brother arrives. I want all three of my sons here for the celebration."

"Celebration?"

"Oh… forgive me, funerals are supposed to be a sad time, aren't they?" His lips lifted into a cold sneer, one that mirrored the lack of empathy in his eyes.

In that moment, I knew that what was about to happen would change all our lives forever. Dread and anxiety rattled through my bones as the chill of the meat locker froze them solid.

"Fuck you!" Sergio hissed, spitting at my father's feet. "The only person who should die in this family is you."

Sergio's head whipped to the side as my father's pistol met with his cheek, creating a gash in his already bruised face.

"You broke my heart, Sergio. I had plans for you—for this familia, and now you have ruined them all because you decided to fuck this little bitch."

He moved to strike the defenseless Catalina, but I intervened, taking the blow for her.

"Stop! You will not strike a defenseless woman!"

His eyes narrowed, slicing through me like a razor wire. "Get out of my way, Emilio!"

"No! This has to stop. I'm not going to let you ruin this familia any more than you already have."

"Me? ME! I've done nothing but keep this family together. It was him that tore us apart!" my father bellowed.

"Shut the fuck up!" Sergio bit back, spitting blood on the floor.

"What? You afraid of your brothers learning the truth about you, Sergio? You think they will still look up to you when they find out what you did?"

"What's he talking about, Sergio?" I asked cautiously, still standing between my father and Catalina.

"It's nothing," Sergio breathed, trying to catch up with his staggered breaths.

"Lies," my father said with glee. "All of you are filled with filthy lies!"

The door to the room opened, and Mateo was pushed in, almost as bruised up as Sergio.

"Excellent! The whole family is here." He looked at me and smirked. "Isn't it funny how both your brothers show up here with bruising and cuts, while you stand there with no marks on you at all? Why do you think that is, Emilio?"

"Because I came willingly, and they put up a fight."

My father clapped his hands together, obviously agreeing with my remark. "The keyword there is *fight*, Emilio. Your brothers are strong Santoyo men, but you, you're nothing but a weak-willed piece of shit that fucks dogs. If you are to take over this family, I need to know that you are willing to fight for it. I can't leave it to him," he said pointing to Sergio, "he fucking betrayed me." He then gestured his head toward Mateo. "And that fucker over there isn't even my goddamn son. He's just a fucking bastard, the whole reason your whore of a mother is dead."

Mateo didn't even flinch. If my father's words affected him, he didn't show it. He stood there in the corner, his blue eyes simmering with unknown emotions, waiting for the next foot to drop.

"Do you know who killed her?" my father asked, turning to me and Mateo. "Do you know who was responsible for burning this familia to the ground?"

"You," I bit out, staring at him without any fear.

"I would never harm the woman I love. Not even after she betrayed me. That blood is not on my hands, but it is on someone else's," he said, laughing evilly. "Isn't that right, Sergio? Tell them… tell them who is responsible for putting a bullet in your mother's head."

My eyes migrated to my brother, who hung his head in defeat. He was chewing on so many raw emotions, ones I could tell were affecting him to his core.

"TELL THEM!" my father ordered. "Or I'll put a bullet between your bitch's eyes.

Sergio weakly looked over at Catalina and dropped his gaze to the ground.

"I did," he whispered.

My father thumped him on the head with the butt of his gun, forcing Sergio to grunt loudly. "Say it so everyone can fucking hear you."

Sergio's head shot up, meeting my father's menacing gaze with one of his own. "I did!" he shouted.

Mateo and I exchanged a quick look, both trying to process this information being relayed.

"Tell them about that night, Sergio. Tell them why you shot your mother in cold blood. Don't get anything wrong, if you do, your precious bitch is dead."

"He took me into a room. You were on the floor playing with a car, Emilio, while Mateo was suckling on Mama's breast, and Mama, well she was sitting there with fear in her eyes as she pleaded for her life. He gave me no choice… Dos vivirán. Uno morirá. Two live. One dies. I was only eleven, I had no idea what he was asking me to do. All I ever wanted was his approval and love. He asked me to make an impossible choice. Shoot one of you or shoot our mother who betrayed us. I didn't want to do it, and her pleas still haunt my dreams. I live with her blood tainting my soul. She was my first kill, the first person I ever put a bullet in." Tears dropped furiously down Sergio's face, refusing to look any of us in the eyes. "I'm so sorry," Sergio cried. "I should've never killed her that night, I should've…" his voice trailed off, leaving the words unfinished and hanging in the air for us to complete. "I was only eleven," he repeated in an emotional whisper.

My father motioned behind me, and two big guards grabbed Mateo, slamming him into a chair next to Catalina. After he was tied up, my father walked over to his desk, pulling out a revolver. He placed three bullets in the chamber, then handed the gun to me.

"I need a new avenging angel. All of these people who sit before you have a target on their heads." He walked over to Esme, pulling her head back until she was looking him in his eyes. "This bitch is worth more dead than alive. Now that you're married to her, all you have to do is put a bullet between her eyes and all that inheritance she gets on her twenty-fourth birthday becomes yours. She doesn't love you… she's not capable of loving anyone, not even herself." He yanked her head back, placing a cruel kiss on her lips. "But man, does she suck a mean dick. I broke this bitch in early as fuck and been grooming her ever since. You can vouch for that, can't you, Sergio?"

"Fuck off," Sergio growled, tears still streaming down his face.

My father walked over to Catalina, placing his hands on her shoulders, who was still knocked out and unmoving. "This bitch thought she could steal my favorite son from me. The daughter of the great José Charro, my biggest mortal enemy. Putting a bullet in her would send him a message. Don't fuck with the Santoyos. You'd look like a God in the eyes of all my men if you could deliver her fucking corpse on his doorstep."

The gun quaked in my hands, everything inside me fighting the rage that was building up like acid in my chest. How did everything get so fucked up? How did it fall on my shoulders to make such an impossible choice? I shot my brother a sympathetic look as my father came to a stop behind him.

"Now this one. This one stung the most. He betrayed the familia by running off with the enemy like he did. He betrayed you and your brother by shooting your mother right between the eyes, taking her life and robbing you of having a mother for all these years. He thought he could elude me, he actually thought he could turn his back on us, but I proved him wrong. I found someone even more crafty than him. It takes a hitman to catch a hitman, and this bastard was easy to find. Mr. X had him here within two days of my proposal. How fucking exciting is that? I really need to put him on my payroll." He took two long steps before smacking Mateo in the back of the head. "And this fucktard doesn't belong. If Sergio had made the right choice back then, this god-awful offspring would've never made it to his first birthday. You could end his life, Emilio, do what your brother couldn't bring himself to do all those years ago. Tres mueren. Uno vive. Three die. One lives. Make your fucking choice and take your place next to me on my throne, we can run this empire together! Who will it be? One of your miserable brothers? The bitch who carries your brother's seed? Or will it be your wife, the woman who will never love you the way you are hoping for? CHOOSE!"

"I can't," I told him, staring at the four people in front of me who all deserved to live.

He raised his gun, pointing it at my head. "Choose or I choose for you."

I stared at my eldest brother, Sergio, his eyes pleading for me to do what we all knew needed to be done. He was ready to fall on the sword for his woman, thus falling on the sword for everyone else, too. He looked at me attentively, and it was as if I could read his mind, and before I could think, I pulled the trigger.

Chapter Eighteen

Sergio howled out in pain, the bullet penetrating his side, very close to his gut.

My father laughed, obviously he found Sergio's pain hilarious, and turned to me, his back facing away from the four people he expected me to kill. "You missed. Goddamn, that was perfect. You really know how to put on a show, Emilio. You had that damn gun aimed at his head and completely missed. Shoot him again, but this time don't miss."

"He didn't fucking miss, Asshole!" Sergio yelled, coming up behind him and curling his massive forearm around our father's throat and squeezing. "He took out the stupid rope your lackeys forgot to secure. I couldn't get out the knot, but Emilio took care of that for me." Our father struggled to breathe, his face turning purple.

Taking the gun, I spun the revolver, pointing it at my father's head. "Let's see what happens first, Julio." Calling him Padre wasn't worth it anymore. He wasn't a father, he was a sick, sadistic fuck, one that didn't belong on this earth. "If you like Russian Roulette so much, then let's play. There are three bullets in these chambers." I spun the gun again. "What do you think will happen first? You passing out, or you surviving me pulling the damn trigger." I pressed it against his temple, Julio's eyes going wide as Sergio increased the pressure around our father's neck.

"One... five... nine." On nine, I pulled the trigger.
CLICK!
Julio's eyes fluttered shut the second I pulled the trigger, then his whole body slumped forward in Sergio's arms, passed the fuck out.

"Tie that motherfucker up," Sergio ordered as he raced over to Catalina who was still unconscious. He checked her over, then turned to me. "We need him alive."

"Why?" Mateo growled.

"Because I want to torture that piece of shit. I want his pain and suffering to be fucking unbearable. He survived Emilio's impromptu game of roulette, what's a few more hours of pain and agony? The motherfucker is going to die, anyway." As he spoke, he untied Mateo and Esme, but kept Catalina slightly tied to the chair so she wouldn't fall to the ground. He never anticipated Mateo's attack until my youngest brother was running straight at him and tackling him to the ground. You could hear Sergio's nose break the second Mateo's fist connected with his face.

"You fucking killed our mother!" he screamed, slamming his fist into Sergio's jaw. "Why did you kill her and not that motherfucker?"

Sergio pushed Mateo, sending him sailing across the room. He landed against the table, creating a loud crash.

"Fucking stop!" I yelled at them, but my two brothers were in a wild tangled grudge match where neither one was relenting. All this commotion was going to bring my father's guards back in, and the second they entered the room we'd all be dead.

I moved toward them, ready to pick them apart when I heard someone say, "Where am I?" It was Catalina. Her head was up, and she was looking around the room disoriented. She looked over at my brothers who were still fighting on the floor. "What's going on?"

"Sergio shot and killed their mother and now Mateo is trying to kill him instead of the unconscious bastard on the floor that fucking deserves it. Basically, nineteen years of aggression are being redirected and coming out in one pathetic, masculine attempt of whose cock is bigger. Hate to break it to you, boys, but where I may have never seen Mateo's cock before, I have seen the other three in the room. Out of all of you, Emilio has the biggest cock in here."

Both Sergio and Mateo stopped their squabbling to look at Esme, who was now free from her binds and stalking toward them. She was pissed. I could see it in her eyes. "That's right, assholes, none of you have as big of a cock as Emilio. So, stop your fucking fighting and help us get the real villain into a chair." She turned around, motioning to the spot on the floor where our father's body should've been.

"What the fuck?" I yelled. "Where the hell did he go?"

Then I felt Sergio punch past me, straight towards the door that was now wide open.

"Sergio! Where the fuck are you going?"

My brother didn't even turn around, he kept moving forward in desperation. I thought it was because he wanted to kill our father, but that's when I noticed the fourth chair was empty.

Catalina was gone.

Chapter Nineteen

All hell broke loose the second Sergio stepped out the door. From every angle, shots were being fired. He couldn't even make it out of the room without a bullet whizzing by his head. He dove back in, slamming the door behind him.

"We're fucked."

"What are we going to do?" I questioned, shooting Mateo and Esme a confused look.

"We're gonna shoot our way out and save my woman." Sergio grabbed both guns and examined them. "Fuck! We only have six bullets."

"Is that a bad thing?"

"There are at least ten men out there. There's no way I'm going to be able to kill them all without getting myself shot in the process. I'm going to have to take them out one by one, and then somehow grab one of their guns on my way. Which one of you is the best shot?" he asked, looking at me and Mateo.

We both pointed at each other, neither one of us confident in our shooting capabilities. Hell, he was still bleeding from the gunshot wound I gave him near his gut. When I shot him, I had meant to aim for the part of the rope furthest away from his skin, but misjudged, shooting him through his side. The wound didn't seem to affect him, he was moving on pure adrenaline, and the need to save his woman from our father.

"Fine, guess I'll dual wield the two guns like a badass in an action film. Stay here until I clear the room. When you hear no more shooting, it's safe to go outside."

"What if the gunshots stop because you're dead?" Esme asked sarcastically.

Sergio rolled his eyes, staring at his former fuck buddy like she grew a second head. He didn't stare at her like a man who once made love to her, he stared at her like a man who was completely over her and her bullshit. I heard what she said to him before I let him out of the room. It was then I knew he needed to be free from his prison. No man deserved to be spoken to that way, and yet, somehow, I had softened that raging bitch inside of her—even if she was still pissed at me right now. If we got out of this alive, I'd explain to her everything, she deserved to know the truth, no matter how hard it was to hear.

Walking to my wife, I took her hand, searching her eyes for any ounce of fear that may linger in them.

"I'm still mad at you," she informed me, but shocked the hell out of me by giving me a deep, seductive kiss. "I didn't want to die without doing that again."

"We're not gonna die, Esme."

"What makes you so sure?"

"Because we haven't had our happily ever after yet." Bending in, I take her lips again, sweeping my lips over hers as the first shot fires off outside the door.

"Seriously, our brother is out there getting shot at, trying to clear a room full of men that want to kill us, and you two decide now is the best time to kiss? What the fuck?" Mateo grumped.

Pulling away from Esme, I smiled at my youngest brother, almost laughing. "One day you'll find a girl you're willing to kiss in the middle of a firefight."

Another two shots fire off, then we hear a man, not Sergio, screaming in pain, instantly silenced by another shot.

"Do you think that's Sergio doing all the shooting?" Esme asked, her voice on edge. "What if he doesn't survive?"

"He'll survive."

"How can you be so sure?" she asked, nuzzling into my shoulder as I pulled her into my embrace.

"Because Sergio is in love with Catalina, and if his love is anything like mine, he'll do anything to protect her, even if it means taking ten men out all by himself."

My words are interrupted by more shooting, then after ten more shots, the door swings open, Sergio looking tired as fuck, covered in blood splatters from head to toe.

"She's gone. FUCK! She's fucking gone!" He dropped to his knees, fisting the two guns in his hand as he clutched and pulled at his hair. Then he slowly rose his bloody face toward the ceiling, letting out a guttural growl, one that made every wall in the room echo and shake.

"CATALINA!" he screamed.

Chapter Twenty

We couldn't return to our father's home. It was like a fortress, and it was definitely where he was keeping Catalina. We were outnumbered, and there was no way the three of us would survive if we hit him head on.

Sergio was a nervous wreck, pacing the living room like a caged beast, ready to unleash hell on whoever unlatched his door. He was all bandaged up, his gunshot wound taken care of by a local nurse, and his nose covered in crisp white bandages. Mateo had definitely broken his nose, but even though he was hurt, Sergio acted like an immortal man, hell bent on saving his woman from the clutches of darkness.

"I'm going to sneak in there and save her."

"You can't, Sergio, that's like signing your own death certificate," Esme argued. "We got to be smarter than him. What is something he would never expect?"

"Emilio to go instead?" Mateo joked.

"Fuck off, Hermano."

"You heard our dear old dad, I'm not his son, remember?"

Sergio stopped his pacing, walking straight over to where Mateo sat, and dropped into a crouching position.

"What?" Mateo asked him.

"Be thankful he isn't your dad. You don't have to live with that vile blood running through your veins like Emilio and I do. You, mi hermano, are still our flesh and blood. Half brother or not, you're still a part of us because you came from our mother. She loved all of us with all her heart. You especially."

"How can you talk about her like you cared about her? You fucking killed her."

Sergio immediately got tears in his eyes, standing up again. "And that's a demon I will always live with, Mateo. I've regretted that decision since the day it happened. I was so young; I had no idea what was going on. He placed the gun in my hand, like he had done so many times before, and forced me to make an impossible choice. It was either spare the life of both of you or kill her. I never thought about turning the gun on him—not once. Not until after I got older and realized what he did, how he manipulated me to do his damn dirty work. I followed his lead for so many years, and it wasn't until I met Catalina that I realized how my footsteps made a path of their own." Sergio turned to Esme. "I know you hate me, but just know that I never meant to hurt you, Esme. I just fell in love… real love… not the fake love we were forced into."

Esme's eyes briefly met mine, and she hung her head in shame. "I'm sorry for the way I treated you that day, Sergio. I lived a jaded life, Julio handled me like a broken marionette doll that he could control and swing in whatever direction. It wasn't until Emilio showed me what it was like to be loved by someone—real love—the kind you have with Catalina, that I was able to step out of that jaded wonderland I was in, and look reality in the face. I never thought I deserved to be loved by someone like that. Love was always something that seemed impossible for someone like me. But now that I know what a vile monster Julio Santoyo can truly be, I'm done following him. I'll find the men who killed my family and get rid of them myself."

A large lump formed in my throat. I've contemplated a million times how to bring up my father's secrets, but it never seemed like the right time. This moment didn't seem like the right time either, but she deserved to know, and now that I wasn't under my father's thumb, morphing from an ally to an enemy, I had to tell her.

"Esme, please sit down," I instructed, guiding her to the couch.

"Emilio? What's going on?"

I dropped to a single knee, grasping her hand. She gasped, probably thinking I was going to propose, forgetting we were already married.

"What are you doing?" she whispered.

"Esme, do you remember when I asked you to trust me, just before all this happened?"

"Yes…"

"The reason I went silent on you those few days wasn't because I was repulsed by you or hated you. My father didn't tell me anything that would ever make me look at you differently."

She stared at me curiously, taking a deep, therapeutic breath. It was almost as if she already knew I was going to drop a major bomb on her. "Okay, then why did you pull away from me?"

Tears were already threatening to fall from my eyes. The emotional turmoil I was going through by sitting on this information was tearing me apart. I didn't want to break her anymore than she already was, but I knew she had a right to know, they all did.

"He told me a long-time family secret, one that directly involved you."

"I don't understand."

"Esme, I don't know how to tell you this, so I'm just going to come right out and tell you. The night your family died… the night my father brought you home in the rain… the night that you got this," I said breathlessly, passing the back of my hand over her beautiful scar. "It wasn't the Ramirez Cartel that hit your family."

"Yes, it was! I saw the damn tattoos."

I nodded. "You did, but they weren't part of the cartel, not anymore. They were scavengers—former members of the cartel that had broken away and formed their own little gang. They had the tattoos because they couldn't remove them. My father, he used that to his advantage… he hired them… he…" my voice broke off as the emotion I felt in my heart overwhelmed me. "He paid them to kill your family."

She gasped. "Oh my god!"

"There's more. He was there, too. He was the one who killed your family. He's the man you've been looking for."

"He killed my father! My little brothers!"

I placed my hand over hers, bringing her clenching fist to my lips. "They were our brothers, too."

"What?"

"Your brothers, they were also my father's sons."

She pulled out of my grasp. "No! It can't be. There's no way…" Tears spilled down her glorious cheeks, creating a slight contrast to her olive skin—a darkened trail of sorrow that soaked into every pore.

"It's true. He told me. He was the one who…" my voice trailed off again, trying to push the thought of what he did to her that night. Forgetting all the horrific details of how he stole her innocence, I redirected my thoughts, focusing on the one that has affected her the most. "He cut your face."

"Why? What kind of sick motherfucker disfigures a teenage girl like that? He… fuck, he seduced me after all that shit. He convinced me he was good, that he loved me. That whole time… the whole time I laid in his bed… he fucking was the one at the root of everything? How is that possible?"

"Because he's a sick man, Esme. The evil inside him is like black sludge. There's no moving it. It just exists."

"Why would he do this to me?" she cried, clutching her cheek with a trembling hand, not able to keep up with her own tears.

"He said you reminded him of our mother… that he couldn't look at you every day and have you remind him of her. So, he cut your face, disfiguring you so that you would never look like her again. Then blamed the hit on Charro… not realizing you knew who the Ramirez Cartel was."

"But why would he do all this? What was the point?"

"Money. Power. That's the only two things he cares about."

Esme shot up to her feet, lunging for the front door. "I'm going to kill him. I'm gonna put a goddamn bullet in his head and keep firing until every bullet I can find is imbedded in that sorry excuse of a man." She fell to the floor, crumbling in a heap of sorrow that was so defeated and broken that she couldn't even keep herself up. She just laid there and cried.

I moved to her side, bringing her up into my lap and just cradled her. "I didn't tell you because he threatened to kill you… to put you through that pain you experienced that night again. I didn't want to do that to you, Esme. Not when you mean everything to me. I didn't tell you because it was the only way to protect you from him. But now there is no protecting. He wants us all dead, and it's only a matter of time before he sends someone here to find us—eliminating us once and for all."

"There's no stopping him, is there?"

Sergio stepped forward. "What if… no… that's way to stupid and risky."

"What?" Mateo asked, coming to a stop next to my brother. "Spit it out. We need any idea you have right now because from where I'm standing, we're fucked. Like not even in the good way. Fucked like someone took a splintered broom handle and shoved it up our asses, fucked."

"You're not wrong," Sergio said, scratching at his chin. "He took Catalina because he knew we would come for her—that I would come for her. She's defenseless against him, and there's no telling what he's doing to her right now. If we don't act now, I don't know what we'll walk into. We have no allies. We're going in blind. We don't have the manpower to stand up to him. We'd need an army… we'd need…" Sergio's eyes widened, and a strange smile passed over his face.

"What?" I asked him, the anticipation building inside my gut.

"In order to take down a villain like our father, you have to hit him with something he would never suspect, something so sinister and brilliant even he wouldn't see it coming."

Mateo's eyes crossed in confusion before his mouth dropped. "Wait, you're not thinking…"

"Indeed I am."

Both of my brothers were talking so cryptically that I had no idea what either of them were thinking about. Being out of the loop was something I had become accustomed to. "Is anyone going to fill me in on this diabolical plan you both seem to have? I'm totally in the dark here."

I clutched Esme to my chest, getting lost in the unshed tears that shimmered over her irises. She was so damn beautiful, and she was all mine. Fuck my dad for ever trying to take her away from me. He would never have her again. Not while I was still breathing.

Sergio dropped a hand on my shoulder, giving it a tight squeeze. "Think about it, Emilio, what's something Padre would never suspect?"

"I dunno, maybe forming an allegiance with Charro?"

"Bingo!" Sergio exclaimed, his eyes dancing wildly. "He'd never see it coming. We'd blindside him. The only way you can bring down a villain is by pitting them against another villain. Besides us, who has the biggest vendetta against Padre? Charro, the same man whose daughter is being held captive right now. It's the perfect plan."

"You're crazy! We wouldn't even get past Charro's gates, he'd kill us on sight—especially you, Sergio. You fucked her and ran off with her. He fucking wants your goddamn blood."

"Fuck, you're right, Hermano. I don't know what else we can do. Charro is the only option we have to defeat Padre without ending up dead." He slumped down on Mateo's couch, looking even more defeated than when he realized our father had gotten away and kidnapped the woman he loved. "We're dead. All of us. There's no stopping him now. Not without Charro."

Mateo cleared his throat, stepping into the middle of the room to get all of our attentions. "I think I may be able to help with that, Sergio."

"With what?"

"I think I can get Charro to align with us without getting us killed."

"How? That man wants every Santoyo man dead. The second you stepped up to his compound gates, he'd put a bullet in your head. It would be a suicide mission," I said, trying to reason with my youngest brother.

Mateo shook his head, disagreeing with us both. "I think you're wrong. I believe he'll let me in."

"Why?" Sergio asked. "What makes you so special?"

"Because I think I may be Charro's son."

Chapter Twenty-One

Is heaven as beautiful as they say? I feel like death is breathing down my neck, ready to suck away my soul and carry me off to the burning embers of hell, far away from you and the rest of my family that I long to be with. There's no repenting away these sins. They're tattooed to my heart like badges of dishonor. Every innocent man I killed because of Julio Santoyo is suffocating me, wearing me down both emotionally and physically. The fight I once had is dwindling. The only thing that keeps me going is Emilio. He's been my rock throughout this whole mess, centering me and holding me in place from spiraling completely out of control.

There hasn't been a night since Emilio told me about my past, that I haven't cried myself to sleep. And despite my incessant sobbing, Emilio still holds me against him, soaking up every wayward tear and showering me with that love only he can give.

It's been three days since Julio escaped and kidnapped Catalina. The boys have this fucked up idea that aligning with a man by the name of Charro will help them get her back, but I'm not so sure. He's just as dangerous as Julio, and who's to say he won't kill us after he gets Catalina?

I don't want to die, Abuelita. I don't want death to take Emilio either. Hell, I don't want any of the Santoyo boys to die. I need them—all of them.

They've been a part of me ever since that night Julio Santoyo decided to strip me of my innocence, break my spirit, and cut away my beauty. The truth is still numbing to me. I want to say it's all made up, that none of that can be true, but deep down in my heart, in those blank recesses of my mind, I can feel that truth breathing life into my memories. Those memories I locked away, doing my best never to remember again. Bits and pieces are coming back to me, and now that the pieces are laid out before me, I'm slowly starting to put back together the complex puzzle of the memories I tried so desperately to forget.

I can remember his hands... it's the same hands that he placed on me a few months later when he sweet-talked me into his bed. I remember other parts of him, too. Parts that I will chop off and feed to a hungry wild boar the first chance I get.

Mateo was supposed to meet with Charro this afternoon, asking—no begging, for his help. We all know he's the only way we'll ever defeat Julio and save Catalina. But Mateo hasn't checked in, and I have this bad feeling that something may have happened to him. I brought it up to Emilio and Sergio, but they both say these things take time.

Pray for us, Abuelita. Pray for Catalina, who's behind enemy lines and in that monster's clutches. If he would do this to me when I was seventeen. I can't even imagine what horrible things he's doing to the daughter of his greatest enemy—the daughter who stole his son's allegiance to him.

Every day we wait is one less chance of her surviving. We've switched locations every morning we've been on the lam, never staying in the same place for too long. But we can't continue living like this. It's exhausting. We have to do something before it's too late.

Julio Santoyo has to die, Abuelita.

And when I face that man once again, I'm going to take great pleasure in burying Papa's dagger into his cold black heart, piercing that inky mass of destruction and chaos and ridding the world of his pathetic existence.

That man will burn in hell. I will send him past the nine circles and straight into a space filled with nothing but brimstone and fire. I want endless agony for him. I want every part of his skin carved out, disfiguring him like he disfigured me all those years ago. Then when he's hanging onto that last breath of life, I want to plunge that dagger into his chest, remove his blackened heart, and pierce it until I'm clutching his last beat in my own bloodied hands.

I know I sound like a monster again, Abuelita, but my mission won't be complete until that sadistic motherfucker is dead. So, pray for me, Abuelita. Pray that God will take pity on all of us as we suit up for battle, ready to fight a war where we are outnumbered and can't win. But most of all, pray that I'll be able to tell Emilio I love him before I die. I haven't been able to say the words out loud to him yet, but he needs to know that I love him... he deserves that.

I don't know what the exact moment was that I fell in love with him, but I do. With every beat of my fractured heart. He's filling up crags and spaces that have been splintered for so long, I forgot they were even there. Anyway, Abuelita, this may be my last entry. My head is telling me that we won't live to see tomorrow, but my heart is clinging onto that last sliver of hope that maybe the underdogs will win, and the villain will be slayed once and for all.

I love you all. Tell the others I may be seeing them all very soon. If Mateo can't pull this off, we're all fucking dead.

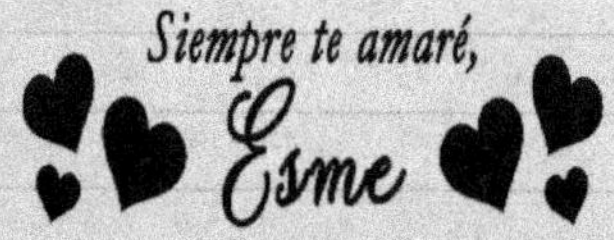

Chapter Twenty-Two

(Maybe an Epilogue of sorts)

She loved me! She actually loved me!

Reading the words on paper was almost as good as hearing them out loud. Even though she was afraid to tell me how she felt, she loved me enough to tell her Abuelita up in heaven. I kept reading over those eight letters, pretending to hear them out loud in my head.

Somehow, I managed to soften her, and even though we were getting ready to walk into the lion's den, I could walk in there knowing that Esmeralda Barrio loved me. That was something a man could die happy knowing. Her love means everything to me. Even more than my own life. I hope I can end this misery she has raging inside her soul—help her finish that mission she's spent a quarter of her life trying to complete.

At this point, his life means nothing to me. He may be family, but his blood is poison, and what do you do with poisonous things? You eradicate them from existence. That's exactly what I plan to do, erase my father so that he can no longer hurt this world with his corruption.

My thumb traced over those eight letters one more time, getting lost in the meaning and happiness they brought to my heart. I was so consumed with that joy that I never heard her enter the room.

She cleared her throat. "Umm, Emilio, what do you think you're doing?"

I couldn't help it, I sprang up from the bed, immediately rushing over to her. Not caring that she caught me reading those private words because I needed to hear them fall off her beautiful lips.

"Say it! Please."

"Say what?" she asked, a slight smirk appearing at the corner of her lips.

"You know what. Say it, Esme, tell me what you know I've been dying to hear since the day we said I do."

She looked up at me, those warm caramel eyes holding my gaze before dropping to my chest.

"You're very handsome."

"Thank you, but you know that I'm looking for something else. Eight letters to be exact."

She laughed. "Have you been reading my journal?"

My eyes darted away sheepishly. "Pretty much since the day you brought it home. Are you mad?"

She shook her head, cupping my cheek with her slender fingers. "Emilio, I've never been good at expressing my feelings or even realizing what they are. That journal helped me get out those emotions I never realized I had bottled up until I emptied the ink onto the paper and let it all go. Did I mean those words on those last few pages? Absolutely. I love you, Emilio. I don't know how or when it happened, but I fell deep and hard for you. You're always there when I need you. You know how to hold me together when I crumble apart. There isn't a single aspect of you that I don't like, except maybe the goodness inside of you that I don't think I deserve. I'm still working on that, the ability to accept your love and feel that I'm worthy of it. If we live through this, I hope you can help me discover that. There's nothing more that I want in this world than to walk the path of life with you for all eternity. I really, from deep down in the depths of my soul, love you."

Our fingers laced together the same time our tongues and mouths met. If we were going to die soon, I was going to go down doing what I do best... making love to Esmeralda Barrio, my wife, my love, my everything.

Our bodies crashed down on the bed, hands fighting to get off any clothing we could. I had barely taken her shirt off when my door burst open and Sergio came flying in, breaking up this intimate moment with his blatant intrusion.

"Sergio? Do you mind?" I asked him, covering my woman from his prying eyes. Not that he hadn't seen her naked before, but now that she was mine, I didn't want a single person to see her beautiful naked body except me.

"I'm sorry, Hermano, Esme, but this is important."

"What's up?"

"It's Mateo. He phoned in to say that he had successfully convinced Charro to help us, and he was on his way here. Then it happened. I was on the phone with him at the time. Oh god! What if he's hurt?"

"When what happened, Sergio? What's going on?"

"There was a huge crash. I heard his car get hit, then I heard an altercation. Someone grabbed him, Emilio... Mateo's been kidnapped."

Mateo

Book Three in the Santoyo Brothers Trilogy
Coming July 20, 2021

Prologue
Mateo

"There he is," a sinister female voice practically sang. She had an accent I couldn't quite place, and the way it filtered into the room was both beautiful and haunting.

I went to move, but I was chained up to a table, cuffs attached to all four of my limbs, my shirt was off, and every inch of exposed skin was covered in something brown and sticky. There was a single, dim light swinging above my head, but the rest of the room was nothing but shadows and blackness.

"What the fuck? What the hell do you think you're doing?"

"What I have to," she said, laughing evilly.

"Who the fuck are you?" I asked in anger, pulling on my restraints as I lunged at the darkness.

She stepped into the light; her blonde hair was like shimmering straw in the faint glow of the dingy bulb. I had to stifle the gasp as her beautiful face came into view. Whoever this girl was, she was fucking gorgeous! My dick had never strained against my zipper as hard as it did looking at her.

"Who I am doesn't matter. What does matter, is the information I need that only you can give me, El Planchazo. The infamous Howler."

I laughed. "You think I'm El Planchazo? Me? Bitch, you're sadly mistaken if you think I'm fucking El Planchazo."

She stepped closer, sticking something to my side. An electric charge ran through my body as the taser connected with every nerve inside of me.

"Don't lie to me!" she screamed. "I know who you are. I've been watching you. I know you're a Santoyo—who your father is. You're all bad men! Men that don't deserve to be in this world," she growled, her accent getting even thicker.

"You're right. I am a Santoyo, but I'm not El Planchazo."

Her brow curled in confusion. "That can't be true. My contact was specific. He said that El Planchazo was a Santoyo son. You are a Santoyo son, aren't you?"

"Yes, I am, but..." She cut off my words with another jolt of electricity. My teeth clattered together noisily as I fought off the pain that seemed to be paralyzing every cell in my body. "Would you stop doing that?"

"Not until I get the information I'm seeking."

"Bitch, I don't know who the fuck you are, but you got the wrong guy. Whatever information you want, I won't have."

"Maybe this will jolt your memory," she seethed, pressing that damn taser against my side again.

"FUCCCCCCK!" I screamed out, body practically launching off the cold metal table. "What the fuck do you want?"

"Where's my brother?"

"What the hell are you talking about?"

"My brother! Where the fuck is my brother?"

"Who the hell is your brother?" This bitch was crazy. I had no idea who her brother was, and I definitely had no flipping clue who she was either. Though, I kinda wanted to know who she was. The way those bright blue eyes shined with fury and rage was quite the turn on for me, even if she was a bit taser happy.

"Arnar! Arnar Björnsson. My beautiful brother. He's missing, and word around town is that your fucked-up father put out the hit on him. So, where the fuck is he?"

"I don't know…" She jabbed the taser in my side again, this time I yelled out in rage, "Damn it, Woman, stop fucking tasing me!"

"Oh, you don't like that, do you? Well, okay, let me accommodate you with something a little more… sweet." She laughed manically as she stepped back into the darkness and reappeared with a small jar of red dotted objects—objects that seemed to be moving.

"What the fuck is that?"

"Oh, these? Thousands of fire ants. These little babies may seem harmless, but when you put a thin layer of syrup all over a person's body, those little fuckers will do everything they can to gobble up every drop of the syrup I just poured all over your body. Imagine tens of thousands of tiny stings, poisoning your body with every damn nibble. I can't even imagine what kind of pain that will be for you."

She started to unscrew the jar, increasing my anxiety as I thought of the tiny little bugs crawling all over me and eating my flesh.

"So, El Planchazo, are you going to tell me where my brother is, or do I have to pull it out of you."

"I told you, Bitch, I don't know shit!" I pulled at my restraints again, only causing her to giggle more.

She opened the jar, pouring a handful of ants onto my stomach. Almost immediately, the most agonizing pain I've ever felt in my life erupted across my torso. Hundreds of painful stings bit into my flesh, as the little assholes crawled over my stomach.

"AHHHHHHH," I yelled out. "Fuck! God, you're one sadistic fucking bitch. Do you know that?"

"Tell me what I want to know, or I'll drop the rest of their friends in for a picnic."

"I don't know anything, I swear!"

Fear gripped me as she tipped the jar, dropping even more ants on my stomach, this time higher up my chest. I couldn't stop screaming. What the hell was wrong with this girl?

"Tell me where my brother is!" she insisted, the ants making a painful meal out of my stomach, getting closer and closer to my face and groin.

The thought of those tiny little bastards crawling up my nose or playing with my junk had me gritting my teeth, fighting the words I couldn't stop myself from saying. "I'm not fucking El Planchazo, okay? But I know where you can find him. Please, just get the ants off me, and I'll tell you everything I know."

She smiled evilly, swatting the ants to the floor and replacing the lid on the jar.

"Good. Now tell me where I can find the bastard."

Other SRS Books

(Click on the Titles of the books below to find other authors and books in the Social Rejects Syndicate)

Taylor Dawn (Scotland) – *Callum*, *Tavish*, *Angus*
Theresa Sederholt (Ireland)- *Ciaràn*, *Patrick*
LC Taylor (Italy) – *Massimo*, *Vincenzo*, *Antonio*
LC Taylor (Chile) - *Matias*, *Cristian*, *Bastian*
Quinn Ryder (Mexico) -*Sergio*, *Emilio*, *Mateo*
Eden Rose (Greece)– *Octavious*, *Milo* , *Emilio*
Beth Hale (United States)- *Mason*, *Dixon*, *Brady*
Janet A. Mota (Portugal)- *Santiago*, *Rodrigo*, *Marco*
Dawn Sullivan (Colombia) - *Tomas*, *Mateo*
KL Ramsey (Albania)- *Llir*, *Altin*, *Veton*
Annelise Reynolds (Russia) – *Nikolai*, *Viktor*, *Konstantin*
A.M. Cosgrove (United Kingdom) – *Jack*, *John*, *Will*
Sahara Roberts (Guyana) – *Kristoff* , *Harlan*
AJ Macey (New Zealand) – *Liam*, *Hunter*
Erin Osborne (Australia*)* – *Flynn*, Lachlan
CR Robertson (Cuba) - *Nicklas*, *Samson*, *Kristian*,

Other Books by Quinn Ryder
The Devil's Armada MC Series

Specter's Wake
The Devil's Armada MC: Book 1

Dusty's Tracks
The Devil's Armada (O.L) Novel: Book 1.5

Cipher's Code
Book Two in the Devil's Armada MC
Coming May 26, 2021

Silent Love
A Devil's Armada Novella
Coming June 7, 2021

The Santoyo Trilogy
Sergio

Emilio

Mateo

Anthologies and Collaborations

Revving For Love: MC Valentine's Anthology
Sinful Valentine

Acknowledgements

First and foremost, I'd like to thank **Taylor Dawn** for creating this amazing universe and allowing me to be a part of it. The Social Rejects Syndicate has been a dream come true for me, and if it wasn't for this woman's strength, tenacity, and drive, it wouldn't be as well put together as it is.

I'd like to thank the amazing beta readers, **Courtnay, Chrystal, Laura, Heidi, Clare, and Michele** that took this book last minute and helped me polish it up and find any lingering pesky errors I might have left behind.

To the **other SRS authors in this universe**. You've all been amazing, thank you for making it so easy to work with others. I truly appreciate you all and everything you bring into this world. It's been a pleasure working for you.

Finally, **to my readers**. Without you guys, these books wouldn't be possible. Thank you for helping this author step into the darkness and loving the dark side along with the light. Love you all.

About the Author

Quinn Ryder lives in a fantasy world full of malicious mafia men, badass bikers, feisty heroines, and chrome that's twitching to rumble between your legs. She's been in the business for over five years, so this author is no stranger to the written word, but she must admit that writing dark material is new to her. Tempted by the corruption and chaos that follows the open road, Quinn created the Devil's Armada after one burly biker refused to leave her head until she finished telling his story. Now, Specter and all of his brothers are ready to suck you in with their rough exteriors, foul mouths, and hearts full of steel and chrome. That world has stretched into the corruption of the mafia, and other dark reads. Are you ready to dive into the world of the Devil's Armada? Come join Quinn Ryder and her men of steel and be prepared to hang on for one hell of a ride!

The Devil's Armada—Don't mess with the Devil if you can't stand the flames.

Quinn Ryder, creating worlds full of danger and intrigue, while riding the road one word at a time.

You can find Quinn on the following social media platforms:

Facebook

Instagram

Twitter

Bookbub

Tik-Tok

Goodreads